A Special Offer Just For You!

Benefit even further from the expertise and accuracy of Peter Leeds. Subscribe to his online penny stock newsletter today!

Your <u>3 year</u> Penny Stock Insider subscription comes with everything listed here:

- 2 new penny stock picks per week
- daily updates
- price targets (buy, sell short term, sell long term)
- 50+ penny stocks on the Hot List
- full research reports on all picks
- Quick Fix reports - Undervalued, Undiscovered, Under $1 (value $29.99 per quarterly report)
- free *Ultimate Stock Pick* audio program, by Peter Leeds ($49 value!)
- many other features and bonuses...

Your one time subscription fee gives you the 2nd year 1/2 price (save $97) and your 3rd year free (save $195)!

All subscriptions come with <u>Instant Online Access!</u> Take advantage of this special offer!

Visit <u>www.PennyStocks.com</u> and click on "Get Started"

<u>Questions? Call or e-mail us anytime.</u>
1.866.MY.LEEDS
Questions@PeterLeeds.com

Visit <u>www.PennyStocks.com</u> for more details.

"We've made hundreds of thousands of dollars in the stock market because of your wonderful leadership and your awesome perspective about the market. I can't believe how much money I am making thanks to you. I will be forever in debt and thankful for all you have done for me and my investment group."   --- Jamil King, Fort Worth, Texas

Welcome Friend and Fellow Investor,

In case you don't have a lot of time to read the book, here is what it says:

1. There is no better way to make a lot of money on the stock market than buying **high quality** penny stocks. Many penny stocks are excellent, healthy companies, which trade for pennies simply because they are small corporations, or that they are being overlooked.

2. Penny stocks are risky. That is why it is so important to do your research and read the opinions of those experienced in this area of the market. There are a few simple measures that anyone can take to avoid the common pitfalls that could cost you.

3. **Only 5% of penny stocks are good enough to make the *"Leeds Analysis"* cut**.

There is a growing trend towards owning penny stocks in quality companies with tremendous upside potential. Sophisticated investors and newcomers are turning to high quality penny stocks, to give their portfolio growth, speed, and excitement. They are turning to Peter Leeds, the Penny Stock Professional.

Questions or comments? Call, e-mail, or visit!

1-866-MY-LEEDS
Questions@PeterLeeds.com
www.PennyStocks.com

Understanding Penny Stocks

Disclaimer and Disclosure

Good! You are reading the disclaimer.

That sets you aside from 80% of the people who will be reading *Understanding Penny Stocks*.

Reading disclaimers is very important when dealing with penny stocks. You have now shown that you are a little (or a lot) wary. Keep that attitude because it will help you avoid many of the dangers and mistakes out there in the penny stock markets.   So, as promised here is our disclaimer:

Understanding Penny Stocks is a wholly owned and copy written property of Modern Strategies Inc. The author and its publisher have received no compensation of any type, or in any form from the stocks and companies featured or mentioned in this publication.

The author is not a registered investment advisor. Readers should not view information found within this book, domain, or any of its reports as offering personalized legal, tax, accounting, or investment related advice.

No comment or opinion in this book should be construed as a recommendation or solicitation to trade any security.

Viewpoints presented are opinion only. Secondary information, when used, is obtained from sources deemed reliable, but the accuracy is not guaranteed. Secondary information sources that provide corporate data are sometimes used during research and the publisher can not verify the accuracy of the data beyond its presentation.

Understanding Penny Stocks® is a heavily copy-written and protected product©.

Understanding Penny Stocks

Here is what I can show you:

1. How to discover the **Big Gainers** before they make their moves.
2. How to **Limit Your Risk** and avoid the dangers.
3. Discover advanced strategies, like **Playing the Volatility** for short-term gains.
4. **How to Buy and Sell**, and get the best prices.
5. Why penny stocks **Pack More Punch** than other types of investments.
6. How to tell **Good Penny Stock Picking Services** from the bad.
7. Discover the top **Insider Secrets** and tricks of the trade.

Capture the Big Gains: I will reveal Leeds Analysis to you, which I use to uncover such explosive penny stocks like DCSR. Just take a quick look at the chart to see the power of penny stocks, as the shares soared from 38 cents towards $10.00!

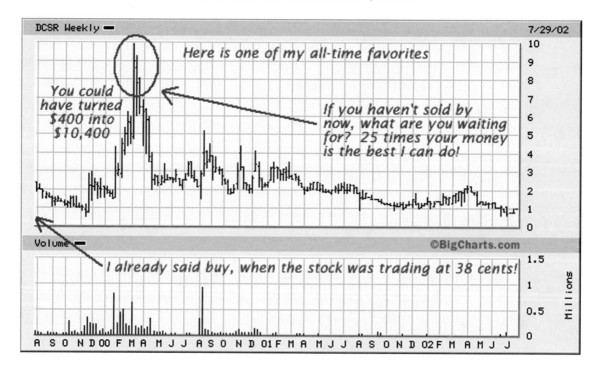

Protect Yourself: I will also show you how to avoid the common pitfalls that cost many penny stock traders money and confidence.

It's Easy to Get Started! If you have never traded a stock before in your life, you will quickly see how easy it is to start buying and selling penny stocks.

Understanding Penny Stocks is the most in-depth, comprehensive look at the exciting world of penny stocks.

The strategies and information I show you can be applied right away, to real-life penny stocks. You may be enjoying your first big profits in a matter of months, or weeks, or days...

Using the techniques detailed in this book, I have built up a fortune from a few hundred dollars. This book is designed to help you do the same.

This book covers every aspect of penny stocks in specific, illustrated detail, so that you can benefit whether you are brand new to investing, or are an experienced trader.

As well, this is the first time these long-secret techniques have been revealed to the public. The details found in the sections on Leeds Analysis are worth their weight in gold.

Enjoy the book, and let me hear from you!

Sincerely,

Peter Leeds, Penny Stock Professional

Age of Penny Stock Traders

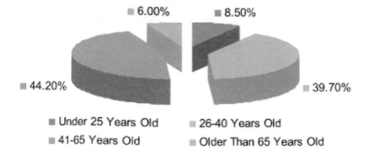

- 6.00%
- 8.50%
- 44.20%
- 39.70%

- Under 25 Years Old
- 26-40 Years Old
- 41-65 Years Old
- Older Than 65 Years Old

Household income of Penny Stock Traders (in thousands)

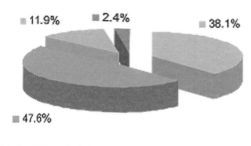

- 11.9%
- 2.4%
- 38.1%
- 47.6%

- Under $50
- $50-$100
- $100-$175
- More than $175

Chapter One:
Your Welcome Letter

Forget everything you know about penny stocks. Forget the things you've heard, forget the experiences you've had, and forget the penny stock profits and losses of your friends and family. *Understanding Penny Stocks* will introduce you to the TRUE world of penny stock investing. A world that is much different than you think.

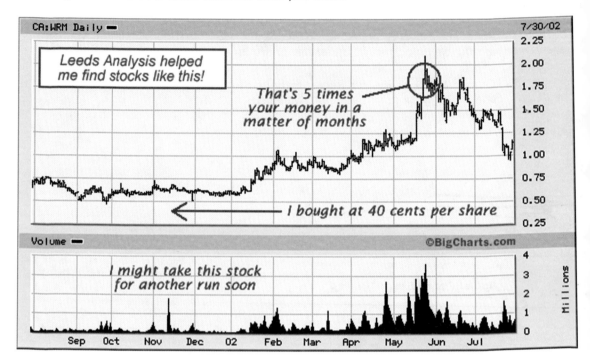

This book will help you become a penny stock machine; avoiding the dangers, knowing the good stocks from the bad, picking opportune buying and selling prices, and taking profits.

After a life dedicated to penny stocks, I forged what I feel to be the single ultimate tool and resource for any level of penny stock trader. That tool is Leeds Analysis, and it helps uncover the big penny stock gainers.

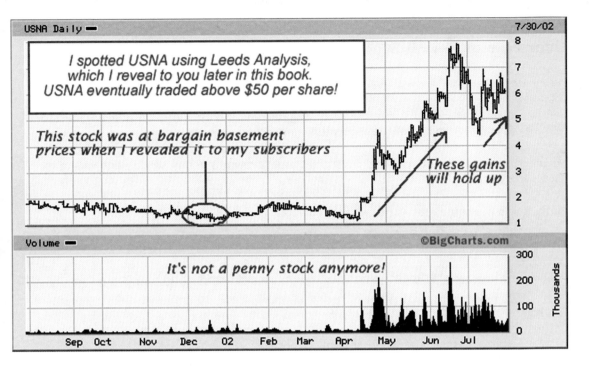

I spotted USNA using Leeds Analysis, which I reveal to you later in this book. USNA eventually traded above $50 per share!

This stock was at bargain basement prices when I revealed it to my subscribers

These gains will hold up

©BigCharts.com

Volume ▬

It's not a penny stock anymore!

I was told that giving away this information was crazy. I was told it was a mistake to let the public know the same research secrets and techniques that literally took myself, and my team of employees years to develop.

And to give it away free!? Boy did I hear it from my business associates!

Was it crazy? A mistake? Perhaps time will tell.

Yet, I still fail to see the harm in revealing these concepts to the public. Penny stocks have been good to me, and I think it is human nature to want to share my excitement with you.

There are concepts and secrets revealed throughout *Understanding Penny Stocks* that I have previously sold for a lot of money. My hope is that you learn from all the effort and work I have personally put into this book, and tell two or three others about this new resource.

I intend to do very little advertising or promotion, and am relying almost exclusively on word of mouth. In other words, I am relying almost exclusively on you.

I hope you like what you read, increase your profits from the exciting world of penny stocks, and encourage a handful of others to stop by and check us out.

Sincerely,

Peter Leeds, Penny Stock Professional
Author of *Understanding Penny Stocks*

Chapter One:
Overview of Penny Stocks

Penny Stocks.

Vehicles of fast fortunes to some, but risky, costly investments to most. For every investor that makes a killing on one of these equities, nine others lose their shirts.

So why the overwhelming interest? Why are people drawn to penny stocks, and willing to accept the risk?

Perhaps it is the same reason people play roulette. However, unlike roulette...

There are ways you can vastly improve your odds of landing the big returns!

You may be amazed that making money in penny stocks (and having fun) is not that difficult.

You just need a secret weapon that can;

1. Introduce you to the world of penny stocks;
2. Reveal long-hidden trading secrets;
3. Give you unfair advantages for picking the best out of these volatile issues.

Happily, you are reading that secret weapon right now.

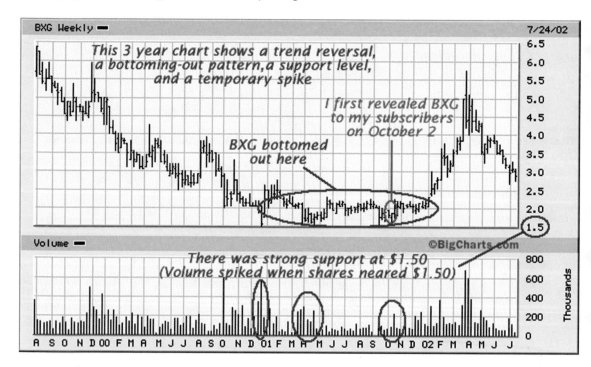

It will require a little commitment and work on your part, but much less than you may think. Meanwhile, the rewards could far and away out pace the required effort.

To put it in perspective, many investors have sunk hundreds or a few thousand into penny stocks and walked away with enough money to buy a house or quit their job or take that dream vacation.

One of the more rewarding unsolicited testimonials I have personally received was an e-mail from a happy client who had attached a picture of the large boat he had bought with his penny stock gains.

Indeed, there is no better feeling than watching your penny stock soar many hundred percent, turning your small investment into a fortune. Sometimes you might make a month's salary from a few hours of work, other times you could turn a small amount of cash into a down payment for a dream home. *Understanding Penny Stocks* will show you how to do this.

$1,000 invested in...	
Diamond Fields becomes...	$41,708
Hixon Gold becomes...	$21,175
Disc Inc. becomes...	$10,868
Colony Pacific becomes...	$43,506
Hampton Court becomes...	$39,000
CompuSoft becomes...	$8,880
Western Pacific becomes...	$20,451
These are just a few examples. **This list could go on for pages and pages...**	

However, it would be foolish to ignore the flip side of penny stock trading, because only naive investors think they can not lose. There are actually dozens of ways to 'lose', most of which are easily avoidable. The trick is to protect your investment money in a way that ensures the gains more than offset the losses.

That is part of the beauty of penny stock investing: You can only lose 100% of the money you invest, but your gains can be unlimited. A $500 investment can become worthless, or increase to $100,000 or more, or anywhere in between.

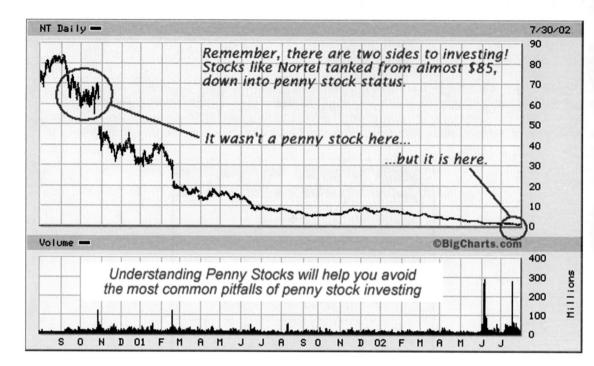

Remember, there are two sides to investing! Stocks like Nortel tanked from almost $85, down into penny stock status.

It wasn't a penny stock here...

...but it is here.

©BigCharts.com

Volume ▬

Understanding Penny Stocks will help you avoid the most common pitfalls of penny stock investing

By reviewing and enjoying this book, you will not only learn where and how to uncover the best penny stocks, but you will also discover the biggest mistakes (which are made even by experienced traders), and how to avoid them. You will be putting yourself into a select group that has the ability to continually reap trading profits.

You will be able to investigate that stock you heard about from a friend at work, tear apart its balance sheet, delineate its market share prospects, rate its management team, and even apply technical analysis to its trading chart to pick the best buying and selling opportunities. I also reveal professional trading secrets that you are not supposed to know about.

The beginner will benefit from square one, learning everything from getting started to picking their own penny stocks. Advanced traders will benefit by applying my ground-breaking analysis strategies.

There is no more complete or comprehensive source of information on penny stocks available anywhere.

I even include my long-secret Leeds Analysis method which will allow you to find the most incredible, undiscovered companies, and pick them up at the most opportune buying prices.

With a little work and the knowledge revealed in this book, you will magnify your odds of reaping monumental returns. Leave the roulette wheel to the suckers. With *Understanding Penny Stocks* you have a secret weapon.

Chapter One:
Credentials for Peter Leeds

So who am I, anyway? My name is Peter Leeds and if you are interested in penny stocks, you may have already heard of me.

For years my company has been involved in the penny stock research and publishing industry.

I developed the first trading methodology specifically for picking penny stocks that was commercially available (through my book, *Stocks That Will Make You Money*), and I enjoy nearly 70% of market share among penny stock publications.

With *Understanding Penny Stocks* you get an in-depth look into my brain, and will benefit from all the industry secrets, insider know-how, and stock-picking techniques that have only come from many years of success. I have been interviewed on television and radio and quoted in the newspapers for my revolutionary theories and approaches to investing in penny stocks. (Recent media coverage includes NBC, CBS, Associated Press, CNNfn, and more...)

In addition, my writing and theories have been incorporated into and displayed upon dozens of different financial websites.

Specialized reports that I have produced vary from *The Hot List, Profit Maker*, and *Platinum Picks* features, to such articles as *Profit Opportunities from the Gold Sector*, *The New Investor Special Report*, and an extensive list of others.

My methods have become so well known that several different financial websites use the Leeds Analysis techniques I have developed, to uncover penny stock picks for their subscribers.

Credentials for Peter Leeds	
Books:	*Dancing With The Dragon (Penny Stock Strategies), Stocks That Will Make You Money*, and now *Understanding Penny Stocks*. Coming soon: *Penny Stock Millionaire*
Live TV and Radio:	NBC, CBS, CNNfn, KPHN Total Business PM Show.
Printed Media:	Barron's, Associated Press, Yahoo! Finance, CBS MarketWatch, LA Times, Newsday.com, Seattle Times, Seattle Post-Intelligencer, News.com Australia, the Boston Globe, and more...
Ongoing Publications:	*The Hot List, Profit Maker, Platinum Picks*, Subscription-based content for nearly 15 different web sites and portals.
Special Reports:	*Profit Opportunities from the Oil Exploration and Production Sector, Profit Opportunities from the Gold Exploration Sector, Getting Started in Penny Stocks, Support Levels and Loss-Minimization, Paper Trading for Risk-Free Investing*, and many, many more...

Regardless of the setting for my work, one thrust has always been towards educating the investor. I have found time and time again that learning about penny stocks from the ground up runs in direct correlation to returns.

I have also noted that impatience, greed, and unrealistic expectations run indirectly to stock market gains. Be forewarned.

Well, one way to educate investors was to release our proprietary Leeds Analysis methods to the public. It was a long and difficult process before I came to that decision, but I strongly believe that I have made the right choice.

The task fell on me many moons ago to pull all of the information together and present it in a clear and understandable way. A way that would benefit you the most. After many long and difficult days, *Understanding Penny Stocks* was finally available.

Now you have a level playing field with the pros, and a hands-down advantage over 95% of penny stock traders.

Chapter One:
About *Understanding Penny Stocks*

From the very basics to more advanced trading concepts, *Understanding Penny Stocks* is a complete resource.

I do mean complete. Whether you want to find out if your grandmother's old stock certificates have any value or you need to know which debt ratio is most effectively applied to the biotechnology industry, I have your answers.

I even take it one step further. For any questions you have, or any concepts that need clarification, send me an e-mail to Understanding@PeterLeeds.com. That way you'll get a first person reply from a professional.

So, what's in *Understanding Penny Stocks* for you?	
Select your level of investment experience:	**How this book will benefit you!**
☐ I have never invested or bought a stock before in my life.	*Understanding Penny Stocks* will introduce you to the entire world of investing. I tell you how to get started, from the very, very beginning, through to when you make those first few trades. And do you know what? It is really not as difficult as you think!
☐ I've traded stocks, but never penny stocks.	There are a few important differences between penny stocks and other types of investments, and I hope you will give me the opportunity to tell you all about it. Once I reveal these very important concepts, you will see that penny stocks are much more fun and potentially rewarding than other types of stocks.

☐ I have traded penny stocks a few times before.	Without proper guidance, most penny stock traders end up losing money. This book reveals the common pitfalls that affect most traders, and describes some long-secret penny stock research techniques that will help you find the most explosive investments out there.
☐ I am very experienced as a penny stock trader.	I provide detailed fundamental and technical analysis techniques that will give any penny stock trader a huge advantage. As well, I will tell you many insider tips and industry secrets in *Understanding Penny Stocks* which were never meant to be revealed!

Understanding Penny Stocks can help you learn the ropes before you risk a dime. I will show you how to prepare for trading these exciting investments, how to uncover your own penny stocks that are about to make their huge moves, and how to trade them profitably.

This book will also help you decide which, if any, of the professional penny stock picking services are the best for you. Learn which resources to use and which to avoid.

From getting your first stock broker and buying your first penny stock to advanced hedging and technical analysis trading strategies, *Understanding Penny Stocks* is a one of a kind resource.

There is no other source of information or secrets for penny stock traders that is even close to the quality and comprehensiveness of this book.

Chapter Two:
All About Penny Stocks

Introducing penny stocks!

This chapter of *Understanding Penny Stocks* tells you everything about these exciting investments and then some! From what they are, to where they trade, from learning the ropes, to how to trade them.

By reading this chapter you will be completely versed in the fun and exciting world of penny stocks.

It all starts with *What Are Penny Stocks*, which is a quick, straight-forward read that you may find enlightening and entertaining.

Chapter Two:
What Are Penny Stocks?

As promised, *Understanding Penny Stocks* starts from the very beginning.

For the purposes of *Understanding Penny Stocks*, I will treat any share that trades under $2.00 as a penny stock.

Strangely, there is no official definition for penny stocks.

There are three different criteria that various individuals and organizations use to define penny stocks. What is considered a penny stock really depends with whom you are dealing.

Penny stocks can be defined by:

1. Price Per Share:
Sometimes any shares that trade under a certain price are considered to be penny stocks. For example, the SEC considers all stocks that trade for less than $5.00 per share to be penny stock. Different individuals and organizations have their own cut-off.

2. Market the Stock Trades Upon:
In some schools of thought, any shares that trade on a certain market (i.e. - the OTC-BB, or the OTC, or the 'Pink Sheets,' or the TSX Venture) are treated as, or considered to be, penny stocks.

3. Market Capitalization:
Market cap is simply the total trading value of the entire company. The value of each share of a stock, multiplied by the total number of shares outstanding, equals the market cap.

For example, 12,343,000 shares of ABC at $0.29 each gives ABC Corp. a market cap of $3,579,470 (12,343,000 shares times $0.29 per share = $3,579,470). That is kind of like saying that the company's total value is 3.5 million dollars.

In some cases, organizations or individuals will treat any company beneath a certain market cap (for example, less than $10 million) as a penny stock.

Interestingly, using option 1 or 3, a company can have its shares change in price moment by moment, and may drop in or out of the definition of 'penny stock' over time. What may be a penny stock when the markets open in the morning may not be a penny stock by noon.

In some cases the definition of penny stock is generated by a combination of the above criteria. For example, any stock trading on the NASDAQ SmallCap *AND* with a market cap of less than $20 million is considered a penny stock.

What is a Penny Stock?	
Defined by price per share:	I treat any share that trades under $2.00 as a penny stock. The Securities and Exchange Commission (SEC) considers any stock below $5.00 per share to be a penny stock.
Defined by the market	Some markets that trade penny stocks include:

The stock trades on:	Over The Counter (OTC) NASDAQ SmallCap Pink Sheets Over the Counter Bulletin Board (OTC-BB) Canadian Venture Exchange (TSX-V)
Defined by Market Capitalization:	Stocks with less than $50 million in total capitalization can be considered penny stocks, but this market cap cut-off varies greatly from one organization's definition to the next.

I have specifically developed my techniques and trading methods to apply to shares less than $2.00 in price.

However, keep the other definitions in mind because what is and is not a penny stock will depend on who you ask. The only common characteristic that we feel holds true from one definition to the next, is that penny stocks are high risk, high reward investments.

Penny stocks are high risk, high reward investments. It is easy to lose money on a penny stock investment. However, if your shares do begin to move, they can produce hundreds of percentage points of gains, and they often do this in only a short time frame.

Penny stocks are often very volatile, and just as often unpredictable.

In most cases, penny stocks are considered to have higher risk and higher potential rewards than most other 'more conventional' investments. Their speculative value can be extreme, and their visibility of information and / or accessibility of operational results are usually very poor.

Few financial professionals venture into the field of penny stocks because they are either unwilling or unable to do the work required to accurately predict what these highly explosive shares may do.

Or perhaps some big-wig investment types feel that low-priced shares are 'beneath' them. Hmmm. I could have retired when I was 26. Is that beneath them?

Chapter Two:
Big Stocks vs. Penny Stocks (Part One)

As you review the following differences between "blue-chip" equities and penny stocks, you may be able to see why professional analysts and institutional investors usually shy away from these speculative shares.

The kind of money that the big players use could crack the backs of many of these penny stock companies. There would not be enough volume on the other side of their trades to enable the transaction, because some penny stocks often trade only a few thousand dollars worth per day.

The negative connotation towards penny stocks among financial industry insiders needs to be kept in context. Sure, these investments are often low-volume, inexpensive shares of unproven companies. However, that is the beauty of penny stocks, and is partly why you can acquire such potentially rewarding stocks at such bargain prices.

As well, the lack of institutional interest is one of the keys to our methodology of picking winning penny stocks. Getting involved early, then holding on as the company gets discovered and explodes in price, is partly dependent upon the previously unknown company suddenly gaining interest from bigger players.

Speculation:

Speculation is based on penny stock companies having lower available information about their operations, minimal revenues, unproven management, and often an unproven product or industry.

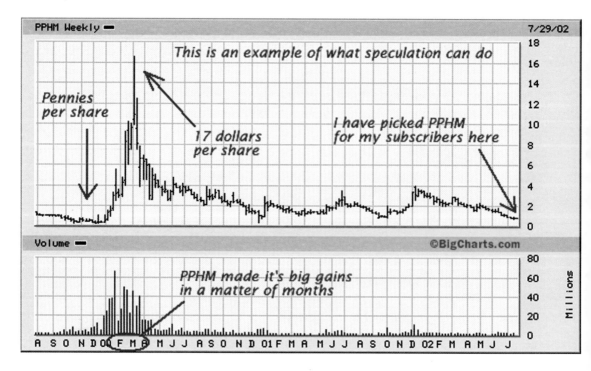

A big-name company like General El... ...Ford Motors will have very little speculative value. In other words, you will r... ...ake hundreds of percentage points on your shares, but instead would ... ... of 10% to 20% per year.

In some cases ... ...to hedge or protect their portfolios, out-perform t' ... ...sify their exposure.

... f selling when you have realized a 20%
... make their gains by the hundreds of

The... ...y stock field, so the best way to succeed is by ...ulative value. The chance of buying into shares ...multiply 10 or 20 or 50 times in price is the whole idea of

Value an... ...ility:

Large-cap companies usually have more predictable revenues and earnings. Many analysts and investors follow the companies, so that day to day events are quickly factored into the share price, and the stock often reflects a pretty accurate 'worth.'

In contrast, it is not possible to calculate the actual worth of most penny stocks. Some do not have inventories, a revenue stream, or even a proven product. The shares rise and fall based on buying and selling demand, and that demand is driven mainly by waves of speculation.

By their nature, it is nearly impossible to know what price a penny stock share should be trading at, and conventional financial ratios and industry comparisons are rarely effective measures for realizing a penny stock's tangible value.

Compare Penny Stocks to More Conventional Blue-Chip Stocks		
	Penny Stocks	**Blue-Chips**
Speculation:	Highly speculative. For some penny stocks, speculation is all they have going. The better penny stock companies often see their shares soar on speculative buying.	Little or no speculative value.
Value and Predictability:	Less actual value, greater perceived potential. Penny stocks are also very unpredictable.	Safer but boring. Very little potential for a price explosion.
Fundamental Analysis and Information Availability:	Poor visibility levels, lower reporting responsibility. Can be researched properly if the Leeds Analysis method I describe in Chapter Three is applied.	Well known, heavily followed companies have a wealth of information available.

Technical Analysis:	TA methods can not be applied to penny stocks, except for the proprietary techniques and indicators I describe in the second half of Leeds Analysis later in this book.	TA can be easily applied to high volume shares.
Volatility:	Highly volatile, with more frequent profit-taking opportunities, and greater price swings.	More secure and insulated from volatility.
Spread:	Sometimes there is a gap between prices of buyers and sellers.	High volume stocks have very little spread between the bid (buying offer) and the ask (selling offer) prices.
Risk / Reward Ratio:	The risks are higher, while the potential rewards are much greater.	Less risk, less reward potential.
Ease of Acquisition:	More complicated to purchase some types of penny stocks, such as those trading Over-The-Counter.	Much easier to trade through your broker, no special commission rates.
Revenues and Company Life-Cycle:	Lower or no actual revenues. Initial or growth stage companies.	Mature or advanced companies, less growth but greater revenue streams.
Dividends:	Very rarely pay or are in the position to pay dividends.	Many blue-chip stocks pay dividends.
Takeover or Acquisition Targets:	More likely to be taken over by another company, which is usually very beneficial to the price of the shares.	More likely to be the company purchasing or taking over the smaller player, which is usually detrimental to the price of shares.
Industry and Sector Influences:	Highly exposed to sector influences, to the potential benefit or detriment of the shares.	Insulated to the impacts of the sector and industry.
Economies of Scale and Niche Marketing:	Niche marketing is more important, because penny stocks can not compete with the economies of scale of the bigger players in their field.	Benefit from economies of scale, but can not respond, react, or adapt to the smaller companies quickly enough. Often leave niches exposed for penny stock companies to capitalize.
Driving Factors vs.	Share price is not strongly tied to	Fundamental results and the

Fiscal Situation:	fundamental results and the balance sheet.	balance sheet are the most important factor to the share price.
Irrational Spikes and Profit Opportunities:	More frequent and extreme spikes and dips, from less provocation.	More stable, less volatile.
Broker Policies:	For certain types of penny stocks, brokers can charge greater commissions, or be problematic.	Brokers will not be problematic for trades in blue chip stocks.
Investment Horizon:	Gains can be seen in short time frames, from hours or days, to weeks or months.	It often takes larger, slow-moving companies years for their share prices to advance meaningfully.

Fundamental Analysis and Information Availability:

Shares trading on senior exchanges must comply with regimented reporting requirements. To keep their shareholders happy, and to maintain their exchange status, they often must detail the entire inner workings and operational finances of their company to the public. It is simple to get the latest results from IBM, and to take it one step further you can even get estimates of future results.

Depending where the penny stock trades, the disclosure level is usually anywhere from mediocre to non-existent. There are penny stock companies which bend over backwards to inform the public of their every move, but these are few and far between.

It will take more work to acquire the information you could easily get from a larger company, and even then the data may not be available.

Chapter Two:
Big Stocks vs. Penny Stocks (Part Two)

Technical Analysis:
Technical analysis is the examination of the trading chart of a stock to look for trends, patterns, and hopefully predict future price direction. For these methods to work accurately, the underlying stock needs to have a high level of trading activity.

The high trading volumes in most large-cap, big name investments make technical analysis of the company's trading chart possible and improve the accuracy of those predictions.

Penny stocks lack the critical mass of trading volume to enable standard technical analysis. For the purposes of penny stock investors, I was forced to develop my own proprietary methods that could be applied to thinly traded securities, and these are detailed in Chapter Three.

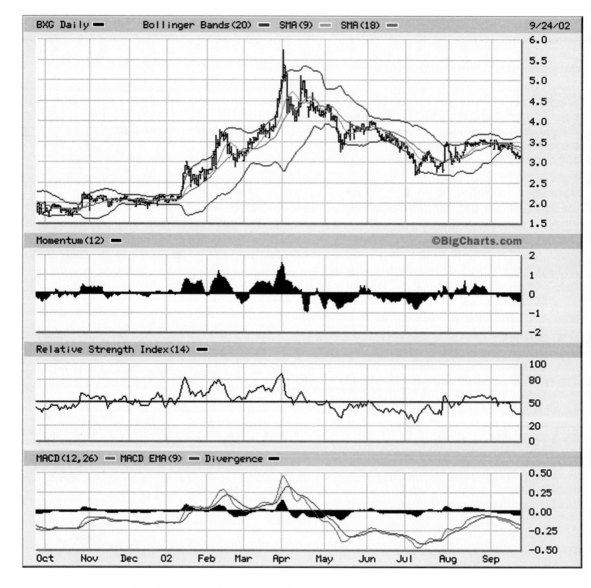

Above is an example of some of the Technical Analysis indicators that can be used to attempt to predict stock price direction.

While they have little bearing on the concepts presented in *Understanding Penny Stocks*, they are presented here as an example. Some of the indicators featured above include smooth moving average, Bollinger Bands, momentum, relative strength index, and others.

Side Note: I did not need to use all this fancy technical analysis to discover BXG (the stock featured above) just before it made its big move. Rather, I found BXG using Leeds Analysis and revealed it to my subscribers just before it multiplied in price.

Volatility:
Penny stocks can often undergo dramatic price swings, and often these moves can be on nothing more than a large buy or sell order. It is not unusual to see your shares drop or spike 20% or 50% or more during a trading day, and even return to their original starting point by the end of that same day.

When a company does come out with a significant press release, for example a biotech gaining FDA approval for its latest drug, expect the shares to make a big move, and even potentially build upon that advance the following few trading days. Price explosions of several hundred percent in a matter of hours or minutes are not uncommon.

Spread:
Stock markets try to match up the highest bid price (to buy shares) and the lowest asking price (to sell shares). When these numbers match a trade takes place. For example, when you see a price quoted as $0.25, you know that the last trade was when a buyer and a seller both agreed upon $0.25 for their transaction.

At all times when the bid and ask are not matching, there is a spread. For example, if the highest bid is $0.80 and the lowest ask is $1.00, the spread between the two will be 20 cents.

You will quickly find that penny stocks are subject to much larger spreads (on a percentage basis) than more heavily traded stocks. It is common to see penny stocks with spreads of 15% to 30% when the buyers and sellers are not agreeing upon a price.

Risk and Reward:
Penny stocks are considered higher risk, because uninformed or unlucky investors have lost money, and quickly.

Sometimes those losses are contained to a fraction of the invested capital, but other times traders lose 100% of their investment (for example, if the company goes bankrupt). Companies ceasing operations, running out of money, and / or closing their doors is much more common among penny stocks than other larger investments.

That is why it is so important to limit your risk, and avoid the common pitfalls that so many investors blindly fall into. *Understanding Penny Stocks* will help you limit your risk significantly.

It is not unlike driving. Driving will always be dangerous. So, drive a Volvo, the safest car, to protect you. Investing will always be dangerous. So, read *Understanding Penny Stocks* to protect you.

Rewards are also much higher (potentially) than with other investment vehicles. Many penny stock companies have just started out, and will one day be huge corporations. The returns a trader could make off of one of these could be enough to live off for years.

Ease of Acquisition for Individuals:
You can buy thousands of shares of penny stocks with a small investment. In contrast, it is not always within the means of an individual to purchase 100 shares of a $40 stock, which means that buying blue chip and large cap equity investments is not always realistic.

As well, if you do have a few thousand dollars it is easier to diversify among a group of penny stock companies, instead of buying only one or two more-expensive blocks of higher priced shares.

Revenues and the Company Life Cycle:
Most companies start off with an idea or business model, raise capital, and implement their operational strategy.

If they get this far, and many don't, they enter their growth phase. In this phase, their revenues go from nil to some level that (usually) is still not enough to meet their expenses.

The growth phase, when companies become discovered by the public and the financial industry, is when they usually enjoy the greatest share price movement.

As a company matures, they begin looking for additional complementary products and services to sell. They get their fiscal situation in order, turning those revenues into earnings, and may even pay dividends.

This process from new company to mature corporation takes years. Microsoft was once a two man operation, and they had an office sign that was scribbled on a piece of cardboard. They enjoyed an explosive and arguably the most dramatic growth phase in the history of the stock market, and now have hit maturity. They do not expect to keep advancing at their explosive rate, and now are looking for alliances and ways to consolidate their industry position.

It is important to know that the majority of penny stocks are in the pre-revenue or very early growth stages. Many do not have revenues, and just as many have yet to prove that their concept or operational strategy has any merit.

Many penny stocks in this infancy stage are 'story stocks,' meaning that they have investor interest because of their potential. They have a great sounding 'story' or idea (for example, a new technology or drug that could revolutionize an industry), but have yet to prove it, or to show that they have a method to capture market share or educate society about their concept.

Dividends:
Some larger companies, or those with higher cash flow, pay a portion of their cash to shareholders. Penny stocks, being cash-strapped and in their growth phase by their very nature as described above in 'Revenues and the company life cycle,' generally do not.

However, it has happened from time to time. I once bought shares in BVR.A on the TSX (Bovar, Toronto Stock Exchange) for $0.14 each. The company decided to unload a large cash position that it had on its books. They paid out a one time dividend of $0.16, which by itself was higher than the original purchase price. (Note: Part of my personal justification for purchasing BVR.A was that they had more cash on hand per share than the current trading price). I had more money than I had originally put in just from the dividend, and I still held the shares!

Takeover or Acquisition Targets:

Since the market capitalization of a penny stock company is lower, they are excellent takeover targets for bigger players in the same field. As well, smaller penny stock companies often merge with one another as a way to increase sales and revenues in a bid to compete with or survive against the bigger industry players.

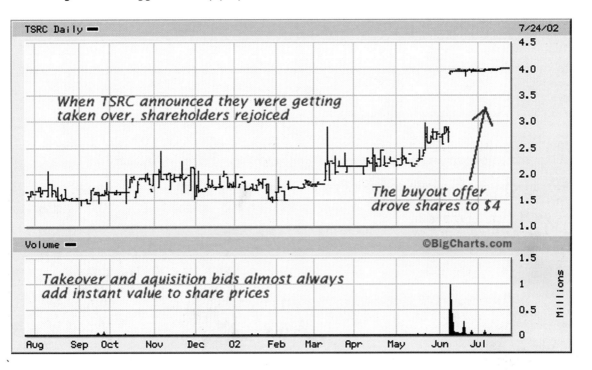

Generally, if a company is getting taken over their share price will benefit. If they are merging with another company, how the share price performs will depend on the situation, and could be beneficial or detrimental.

Chapter Two:
Big Stocks vs. Penny Stocks (Part Three)

Industry and Sector Influences:
While Disney (DIS on NYSE) may be impacted by trends in movie goers, travelers, and advertising, the day to day and month to month changes in these underlying criteria do not sway the stock too dramatically.

In comparison, most penny stock companies have exposure to one facet of the economy, and are highly leveraged against that driving force. Gold penny mining stocks suffer extreme swings as the price of the precious metal fluctuates, and a biotech company could be crushed if a competitor releases a superior drug.

In other words, penny stock companies are usually one-tiered, highly leveraged entities that suffer and enjoy extreme price fluctuations whenever their underlying industry shifts.

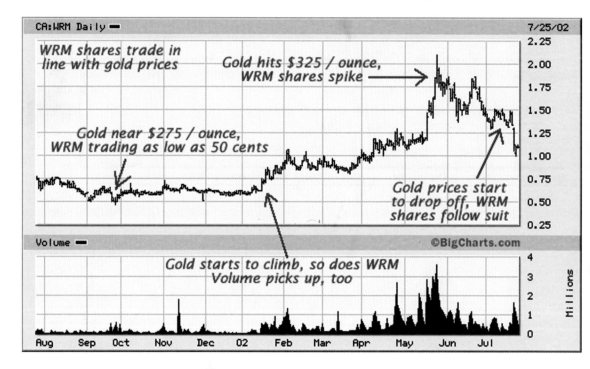

Economies of Scale and Niche Marketing:
Larger companies have more resources and capital at their disposal, and usually enjoy stronger strategic alliances with bigger companies, as well as more pervasive name recognition for their product or service.

This creates problems for penny stock companies looking to enter a pre-existing market that already has a dominant force. In these scenarios, the penny stock company generally performs best by capturing a niche market, rather than going head to head with a competitor.

For example, take a look at one of my favorite stocks in recent years. Paravant Computers had no hope of surviving a market share war with Dell, Compaq, IBM, and all the other players in their saturated sector. However, since they were in the niche market of developing rugged laptops and computer peripherals for outdoor and military use, the company thrived and the stock soared. They enjoyed better earnings and lower debt loads than all of their bigger competitors, and developed name recognition and reputation in the niche market that mattered to them.

Several times over the years I had told members of PeterLeeds.com all about Paravant, and they made money on it each time. After the terrorist attacks of September 11th, 2001 PVAT soared as military spending increased.

Driving Factors vs. Fiscal Situation:

Penny stocks often have too much debt, no revenues, or ugly balance sheets. Looking closely at their fiscal results can be frightening. However, investors often ignore the fundamentals of speculative companies, because of the potential the shares could enjoy if the company's product catches on.

For example, Xerox once had a horrible financial situation when they first started out. However, that didn't matter much, once their technology became the standard - long before they were actually turning a profit.

Irrational Spikes and Profit Opportunities:

Penny stocks can often spike (or drop) based on the slightest provocation, even if that driving factor is of little significance.

Pretend that a change in CEO seems like a great turn of events for an anxious trader, who disliked the old CEO. The investor dives into the market for $10,000 worth of shares, which could result in a 50% leap in share prices because of the buying pressure. However, the new CEO may not be enough to justify a 50% increase in the overall value and market cap of the corporation.

Part of the process is to understand which driving factors are accurately priced into the shares. If you do not share our exuberant investor's faith in the new CEO, you may want to take this opportunity to exit your position and take profits as the stock spikes 50% higher.

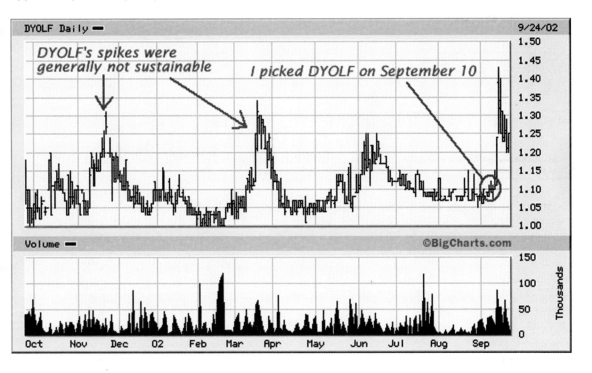

Broker Policies:
Due to the lack of visibility of penny stocks, the markets they trade upon, their volatility, and their risk factors, some brokerage houses have instituted strict policies for trading these investments.

Shares that they consider 'penny stocks,' which are usually stocks for $5.00 and under, are not option eligible. This means that you can not sell short, set stop loss orders, or buy on margin. For most traders this would not be an issue anyway, because these are all more exotic trading methods, and ones that I strongly warn against.

As well, depending on the stock exchange that the shares are listed on, you may not be able to use limit orders to buy or sell, and will have to take the best available market price. There is much more on buying and selling coming up later in this chapter.

Investment Horizon:
Traders generally tend to hold penny stocks for shorter time frames, and attempt to get their returns from the stock in a matter of months rather than years.

Chapter Two:
Why Trade Penny Stocks?

There are many reasons why a trader may get involved in penny stocks.

Sometimes a new investor will want to learn the basics of buying and selling shares, and low-priced investments seem to be a good place to start.

Sometimes an advanced trader will get involved in these speculative issues to hedge a position, or play with some risk money.

Perhaps you may even have inside knowledge of the prospects and potential of a company you work at, and you would invest in their stock before the business really takes off.

Penny stocks are fun and exciting, which is why some people get involved. Kind of like a high-stakes hobby.

But let me be blunt. Based on my experiences from many years in the industry, the main reason people get involved with penny stocks is to try and get rich.

Of course, any combination of the above factors can act together to drive people into the penny stock markets.

What are your reasons for getting involved in penny stocks?		
☐ Excitement / Enjoyment	☐ To make money	☐ You have some inside or specialized knowledge that you can profit from
☐ You have a strong belief in a concept or idea of a company, you think the stock will explode in price	☐ You don't want to miss the boat, while others are getting involved	☐ You want to increase your portfolio's risk/reward exposure
☐ To learn the ropes of penny stock trading, or just of trading in general	☐ You think you know how to pick winning stocks	☐ A more expensive stock you held took a price dive, and now you are holding a 'penny stock' unintentionally
☐ To increase your portfolio's diversity and exposure to certain sectors	☐ For the purposes of hedging strategies	☐ Other

Are Penny Stocks For Me?

The suitability of penny stocks as an investment vehicle will depend on many factors, and only you can ascertain if they are appropriate for you. Factors affecting your situation will include, but will not be limited to:

- Your risk tolerance
- Your financial and investment position
- The aggressiveness of your trading goals
- Your expectations of returns
- Your level of investment experience.

Chapter Two:
Where Do Penny Stocks Trade?

Penny stocks trade in many places. Some stock markets are very good for trading penny stocks, while others are very dangerous to investors. At the same time, some sources of penny stocks are reliable and trustworthy, while other sources are very risky.

I have always been a proponent of trading in penny stocks, but there are some markets that even I wouldn't go near.

NASDAQ SmallCap Market:

This is both the safest and best place to find penny stocks.

Companies listed here have regimented reporting requirements, and must keep in compliance with these to maintain their listing. This enables investors to have access to the company's financial results and ongoing reports.

Usually, the shares listed here will be $1.00 and up. If the shares of a company on the NASDAQ SmallCap begins trading for less than $1.00, the exchange usually boots these stocks, forcing them to drop down to trade on the OTC-BB (see below).

Most financial quote and news services cover shares on the NASDAQ SmallCap market, so it enables greater information visibility.

As well, the increased visibility will improve trading volume and investor participation. Your brokers will have no trouble enabling your trades in NASDAQ SmallCap shares, and probably won't have any additional commissions or rules for trading these issues.

Shares on the NASDAQ usually have four-letter ticker symbols, such as PVAT, IDEV, and DRAX.

OTC-BB (Over-The-Counter Bulletin Board):

The OTC Bulletin Board (OTC-BB) is a regulated quotation service that displays real-time quotes, last-sale prices, and volume information in over-the-counter (OTC) equity securities.

An OTC-BB equity security generally is any equity that is not listed or traded on NASDAQ or a national securities exchange. In other words, it is a system for creating some regulation and accountability for stocks "without a home."

- The OTCBB provides access to more than 3,600 securities;
- Includes more than 330 participating Market Makers;
- Electronically transmits real-time quote, price, and volume information;
- Displays indications of interest and prior-day trading activity.

OTC (Over-The-Counter):

Different from the OTC-BB, Over-The-Counter stocks refers to any issue that is not traded on a regulated exchange. Some of these sources are detailed below, such as shares you may buy from a phone salesman, or those you could get straight from the companies themselves.

OTC issues are pretty easy to buy, but are nearly impossible to sell, even if the stock jumps up in price. Unrealized profit is worthless. Just about the only way to make money on an OTC stock is to hope it eventually gets listed on a stock exchange, at which point you could sell when you wanted. I estimate that about 2 out of 100 OTC companies actually end up getting a listing on a legitimate stock exchange. I highly discourage buying shares in anything that is considered OTC.

AMEX:

The American Stock Exchange, like the NASDAQ SmallCap, is an excellent source of penny stocks. You will find that shares trading here may have less volume than those on the NASDAQ SmallCap, but the companies are subject to reporting requirements and are followed by much news and quote services, so investors enjoy the same benefits derived from the SmallCap exchange.

Your broker will have no trouble trading in AMEX shares.

Pink Sheets:

Do not buy these ever. The pink sheets are stocks that trade without any reporting requirements or regulation, and have no responsibility to you, the investor. They are very hard to buy and sell, as the trading activity in them is very low and sporadic.

The origins of the Pink Sheets go back to 1904, when the National Quotation Bureau began as a paper-based, inter-dealer quotation service linking competing market makers in OTC securities across the country. Since that time, the Pink Sheets and the Yellow Sheets have been the central resource for trading information in OTC stocks and bonds.

There are no listing requirements. There are no rules. Anything goes. This is what the stock market would be like in a post-apocalyptic world.

Straight from Companies:

It is possible to buy shares directly from the companies in some cases. The main reason to do this would be to avoid paying a brokerage commission. As well, it may be an easier way to acquire shares in a more obscure company than trading for them Over-The-Counter.

Besides the fact that I discourage trading in Over-The-Counter stocks, there are inherent problems with direct purchasing. There can be no assurances that you are getting a fair valuation based on prevailing market prices, and in most cases the quoted amount will be higher than you would have had to pay if buying on an exchange.

For thinly traded Over-The-Counter equities, it may be near impossible to get appropriate trading prices. OTC issues do not have any system of matching up buy and sell orders, so buying the shares is no different than buying a used car. The seller may be asking far too much, and perhaps far more than the most recent trades. The point is that you would have no way of knowing.

Over The Phone: (or by E-mail!!!)

Although it was more prevalent in the '70s and '80s, phone salesmen touting stock should be considered dangerous.

Under no circumstances should any investor accept an offer to purchase shares in a company that they heard about through an unsolicited phone call.

Be sure to watch the movie, "Boiler Room" to get a feel for how these scams operate. I highly recommend this movie, which will help drive the point home.

The companies are promoted aggressively, and in most cases are nearly non-existent, poorly run, fundamentally vacant shells. It is nearly impossible to resell shares in these equities, whether you have made a profit or a loss.

The promoters will be pressuring you with a time frame, and may demand immediate action. The stories of the promoted stocks border on incredible, and certainly if their product or service is embraced by the public, the shares will skyrocket, and the industry will be revolutionized... or so they say! Hang up the phone. Don't say anything - just hang up.

For those that ignore this clear and precise warning, you will deserve the returns these stocks provide you with.

Canadian Markets:

The Toronto Stock Exchange (TSX) and Canadian Venture Exchange (TSX-V) both list penny stock shares, some as low as a couple of cents. If your broker allows for over the border trades, we highly recommend getting involved with Canadian penny stocks. These companies are often trading so inexpensively simply because they are smaller in size (as opposed to being extreme long shots, or highly speculative). With Canadian penny stocks, there are literally thousands of good companies to choose between.

 **Safe Source of Penny Stocks**

 **Dangerous Source of Penny Stocks**

Where Penny Stocks Trade	
NASDAQ SmallCap Market • Excellent investor visibility • Strict reporting and corporate responsibility standards • Easy to buy and sell • Easy to get information and data about the company	**NASDAQ OTC-BB** • Poor visibility • Low, problematic trading volumes • Easy to buy, hard to sell even if they have gone up in price • Little corporate responsibility

AMEX • Excellent investor visibility • Strict reporting and corporate responsibility standards • Easy to buy and sell • Easy to get information and data about the company	**Over-The-Counter** • Never buy OTC stocks • No visibility • Non-existent trading volume • Easy to buy, virtually impossible to sell even if they have gone up in price • Little corporate responsibility • Prices you pay for shares are arbitrary and dictated by the seller
Pink Sheets • Never buy pink sheet stocks • Non-existent reporting and corporate responsibility standards • Easy to buy and very difficult to sell • No information or data about the company, or about the trading activity/prices of the shares	**Directly from the Companies** • Never buy directly! • No brokerage commission charge • Probably non-existent trading volumes • Easy to buy, probably impossible to sell - the company will not even buy them back! • No corporate responsibility requirements whatsoever!
From a Phone Salesman/Woman • Don't even think about it! • Non-existent reporting and corporate responsibility standards • Potentially non-existent company • Easy to buy and impossible to sell • No information or data about the company, or about the trading activity/prices of the shares • Prices are arbitrary and baseless • You are almost certainly being lied to, or aggressively mis-led	**Canadian Markets (TSX, TSX Venture)** • Huge selection of penny stocks • Potentially higher brokerage trading fees • Good reporting requirements and corporate responsibility • Good to medium availability to corporate data/information • Ease of access to trading and pricing data • Easy to buy and sell • Good trading volume in most cases

It is very important to notice the difference between Over the Counter stocks (to avoid) and Over the Counter Bulletin-Board stocks (OTC-BB) which are OK. They sound similar, but only OTC-BB stocks are good to get involved with.

Chapter Two:
Getting Started in Penny Stocks

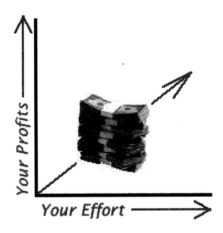

While trading is really quite simple, and most people are anxious to dive right in, I think you should hold off for just a few minutes to make sure you are introduced to the following steps and concepts.

1. First, make sure to read and review *Understanding Penny Stocks* from front to back.

There is no rush to start trading before you fully understand what you want to do, and how to do it. This book can help you prepare, so that you avoid costly mistakes and make some big gains. A few hours of reading could make a big difference.

There is no other source that can introduce you to penny stocks, prepare you for trading, and enable you to uncover winning investments as well. The scope and detail provided is unmatched.

2. Familiarize yourself with general investing terms and concepts, and especially those that are specific to penny stocks.

Always remember that penny stocks follow different rules than other types of conventional investments, and therefore have their own language. You will pick up everything you need to know as you proceed through *this* book.

3. Always get involved in penny stocks at first by paper trading.

It is an easy, realistic method of learning the ins and outs, and you do not risk a dime. I have included an extensive look at paper trading to help even the newest investor gain confidence and an understanding of the penny stock markets.

4. Decide on and document your objectives.

Are you just trying to have fun with some risk money, or do you want to make certain returns in a certain time frame? If you do not have goals, you will not accomplish them.

If you do not know where you are going, any path will take you there!

Set your penny stock trading objectives in advance and write them down. (I am serious about this. You will be amazed at the difference this one step will make!)

5. Decide on your favorite types of stocks (if you have any).

Know the markets you will trade upon, the price range of shares that interest you, the industry groups you like (i.e.-biotech, technology, resources, transportation, etc...), and any other parameters that you feel are significant.

6. Decide how you will go about researching, monitoring, and trading shares.

Are you excited about doing your own research, or would you rather get professional penny stock picks from a service like PeterLeeds.com? What information sources will provide you with the details you need to make a trading decision, and what will those details be?

7. Decide on a broker if you do not already have one.

Open an account with the money you intend to invest. You can do this by reviewing my detailed look at the **Top Brokers for Penny Stock Traders**, included later in this book.

Seven Steps to Starting Out in Penny Stocks
1. Read *Understanding Penny Stocks*
2. Learn the language of penny stocks
3. Start by Paper Trading
4. Decide on your goals and objectives
5. Choose your favorite stocks, markets, and sectors
6. Develop a research plan or choose an alternative approach to getting your stock picks
7. Choose a stock broker

Chapter Two:
Learning the Ropes

Before you begin on what may be a fast-paced, highly volatile endeavor, you must make sure that you properly 'learn the ropes.' Going in without the proper preparation would be a mistake, especially since everything you need is right here in front of you.

So what are the ropes? What do you need to know about penny stocks before you dive in?

I have identified five areas that all new investors should understand.

The 5 Ropes of Penny Stocks
1. The Language
2. The Details
3. Past History and Past Results
4. Future Expectations
5. The Science of Trading

The Language:

As we have already mentioned, penny stock investing has its own language. You should learn this, as well as the basic investing-talk that applies to all stocks. Browse our glossary before you begin, then continue to reference it for any term you are not confident about.

The Details:

For every trade, certain details will be required of you. For example, you will need to know if you are buying or selling, the ticker symbol of the stock (and perhaps the name of the company), the market the stock trades on, and several other points. These requirements are explained in full in the section on buying penny stocks.

Past History and Past Results:

To truly have clarity of what may be ahead for your penny stock investments, you need to know what has happened before.

In general, penny stock trading is just a handful of different scenarios that play out again and again over the generations. Anyone who tells you that old economy rules do not apply to new economy stocks is mistaken.

Review the section on past trends. As well, the chapter on Case Studies imparts many of the lessons I have learned from years of experience.

Going forward without looking back dooms you to mistakes that have already been made a thousand times.

Future Expectations:

There will be differences in the coming years and decades, which will not mimic the past. For example, we expect penny stock investments to become more mainstream, and to begin to shed many of the negative connotations that surround them. Better investor protection methods, as well as more access to information on the underlying companies, will help this transition along.

I present a few personal opinions of what may be to come in one of the bonus sections, called Penny Stock Prophecies.

I also expect that no matter how much the game changes, people will still get burned by greed more than any other factor.

The Science of Trading:

You must understand how a trade happens. Besides your part in the scenario, you should also learn how the exchanges work, what is going on behind the scenes, and how one person's profit is often another person's loss. All of this information is provided in upcoming sections of *Understanding Penny Stocks*.

Chapter Two:
Paper Trading

Paper trading is simply keeping track of imaginary money in real investments. The idea is to find out how you would have fared if you had really traded the stocks with real money. It helps you learn the ropes without risking a dime.

For example, you might want to start with a portfolio of $100,000 of imaginary money, and invest it into your favorite penny stocks. Over time you could trade in and out of your positions, keeping regimented notes of what you have gained and lost.

After your paper trading exercise has expired, you can look back and see how you fared, where you made the most money, and which strategies worked.

Why paper trade?

1. You can learn the ropes of investing, including choosing and monitoring stocks, and deciding on your entry and exit prices.

2. To develop an investment strategy or methodology.

3. To test or refine an existing investment strategy or information source.

4. To keep an eye on stocks that interest you, with the purpose of uncovering accumulation or sale opportunities.

5. For fun.

6. To decide upon the best sources of information, quotes, charts, news, and tracking.

Why Paper Trade?
To learn
To develop a trading strategy
To test a trading strategy
To find buy and sell opportunities
To have fun
To uncover the best data sources

There are any number of ways that you can start up and monitor your own paper trading strategy. What I describe here will simply be the approaches that have had the best results in the past and have garnered the most positive feedback.

However, before you decide on an approach you first need to decide on what your results should be from the exercise:

• Are you trying to uncover stocks to invest in?
• Are you testing a new investment methodology and want to see what results you can attain with it?
• Do you just want to learn how to trade penny stocks?

Your answers to these questions may influence your paper trading parameters.

There are several parameters that can be customized to your own personal preferences. Each should be adjusted to be as realistic to your own personal investment situation as possible. For example, starting with $10 million in cash may yield very different results than what you eventually may get from your real $2,000 investment. Yet, if you only paper trade with $2,000, you won't learn as much because you will do fewer trades.

Starting Cash:

Generally begin with enough cash to let you get a feel for the market, and experiment with several different stocks.

If you have $1,000 real money to eventually invest, and you know that you will be putting that into two different penny stocks, you will certainly need to be highly selective in your choice of stocks.

Therefore, you will also want to encourage a paper trading strategy that forces you to be highly selective while you are learning the ropes, so that the jump to real trading will be relatively parallel.

However, if you keep the imaginary cash level too low, you may not get involved with very many paper trading decisions. Thus, you may not learn very much from the exercise.

I feel that traders should start with between 20 and 50 times their real money level for paper trading. If you eventually will be using $3,000 to invest, an imaginary starting level of $60,000 cash would be appropriate to trade many different stocks, without becoming too unrealistic.

I also believe that, especially for penny stocks, you should have a minimum of $10,000 imaginary starting cash.

Keep the amount a nice, round number so that it is easy to tell if you are up or down, and by how much.

Time frame:

Decide when the paper trading exercise will begin and end. This enables you to see how much money you could have made or lost within a set time period.

Note that paper trading exercises do not have to end at all. Instead, you can see how your stocks have fared month by month, year by year, indefinitely.

I suggest that you paper trade for many months before getting involved in the markets with your actual cash. At the same time I understand that you will be very anxious and excited to begin making these trades with real money, especially if your strategies are paying off.

Decide on These Parameters:
Starting Cash
Time frame
Screening (Criteria for Stocks)
Pricing (Recording of Transaction Prices)
Trading Activity Parameters / Rules
Stock Monitoring Methods
Paper Trading Tracking Methods

Screening:

You may want to limit the theater of paper trading, by only looking at certain stocks on certain markets, or only buying into shares that are below a certain price point. Alternatively, you may decide to have the pool of potential stocks literally unlimited, just as it is in real life.

I suggest that you do not use OTC issues for paper trading, because as I explain earlier, you may not be able to sell your shares when you want. Just because the quote is $1.55 does not mean that you would be able to sell your shares at that price, or at all, so it may create misleading results in your paper trading.

Screening can be done by choosing;

• The price of the stocks you will be paper trading;
• The market that you will focus upon;
• A specific industry or sector (i.e.-no biotech stocks, heavy weighting of Internet issues, etc...).

It is based mainly on your own preferences and should be in line with the stocks you will eventually be trading. Of course, I also understand that you may not know what types of stocks interest you yet. Hopefully paper trading will give you a feel for many different industries, markets, and prices of stocks.

Trading Prices:

Decide on your method of recording share prices for your trades. During any given trading day shares open at a certain level, move around between an upper and lower threshold for the day, and then close somewhere within that range.

If you are trading for real, you can know the price you paid for shares because it will be part of your trade receipt. You will be able to access it through your online broker, and you may have even used a limit order to set the price of the trade. (Limit orders and everything to do with buying and selling will be explained very shortly).

With paper trading you will not have that luxury. You need to choose the meter you will use to gauge the prices of the stocks you trade. For example, you may decide that you will use the **day's closing price** for each stock, whether you are buying or selling. You decide to buy 5,000 shares of TMED on Tuesday, so you take Tuesday's closing price for TMED to calculate how much the 5,000 shares cost you.

While the above example is the easiest for tracking purposes, it is the most unrealistic. If you have the time to check stock prices throughout the day, you may want to instantly check the price the shares are trading at as soon as you make your buy or sell decision.

Other markers you could use would be intraday high or low, the day's average price, or the opening price. These all sacrifice some realism for the sake of simplicity, and may cause aberrations when you apply your strategy to real money situations.

If you are thinking about using limit orders, which you should be, make a note of your buy or sell limit price upon deciding to make a trade. Then at the end of the day see if the shares hit your target price.

For example, you decide to buy 5,000 ABC at $1.15 or lower. You later check and see that the shares hit $1.10 at one point, so you record the purchase of 5,000 shares at $1.15.

If the shares had never hit your limit price (say the lowest price on the day was $1.20), your $1.15 limit order would never have gotten filled. (Meaning, you wouldn't have bought any stock). Simply mark it up as an attempted purchase, and look to the following trading day to try again.

Trading Activity:

Decide if you will allow trading in and out of stocks. For example, you buy a stock that goes up 30 percent, and then you sell it and re-invest that amount into two other stocks.

I do not see any reason you should not be able to sell your shares, take the cash and reinvest. Just be sure to keep extensive notes, and charge a realistic broker commission for every trade.

Monitoring:

Decide ahead of time how you will monitor the stocks you are following. It should be the same sources throughout the exercise, and should also be the sources you will be using once you begin trading with real money.

If your purpose for paper trading is partially to decide on which sources are best, then try them all. Just keep track of which you were using so you will be able to look back later and decide which proved most useful, and more importantly most accurate.

Tracking:

To fully benefit, you will need to keep extensive notes on your paper trading exercise. Keep everything recorded, so you can look back to uncover which trading strategies worked best.

Make notes on the following criteria and instances:

1. Starting cash.

2. Starting time frame.

3. Ending time frame, if any.

4. Any screens, limiting the stocks you can include in your portfolio.

5. Starting value of all the major markets, including NASDAQ, NYSE, and AMEX.

6. All buy and sell orders that get filled, including the stock you bought, the volume, the price per share, the total cost, and your imaginary broker fees.

7. All buy and sell orders that do not get filled, including the stock you attempted to buy, your limit price, and the volume of shares.

8. During the exercise, keep track of the value of stocks and remaining cash at scheduled intervals (for example, every month on the first day).

9. By completing point 1 above, you will be able to easily track your results. If you started off with $10,000 and a month later have $11,245 you will know that your paper trading strategy has netted you 12.45% in only one month.

Keep notes of your portfolio value each time you calculate it, so that you can see not only how your stocks have performed since you started the exercise, but how they have performed from one check to the next.

Keep in mind that you are not only trying to compare your results against your starting value, but also against the market and the underlying sectors in general. If the stock markets have dropped 15% since you started the exercise, but your portfolio has dropped only 2%, you can know that you are out-performing the markets.

Do not forget to take off brokerage commissions for each trade. If you have a stock broker, check to see how much they would charge you for each transaction, based on the volume, price of shares, and overall cost. Remember that limit orders are usually more expensive than market orders. Make notes of the commissions you took off your portfolio, and how you calculated each. Alternatively you could use a realistic number like $15 per trade if you are not sure what your broker will charge.

Paper Trading Checklist:

Start Date: _____

My Goals for this Exercise Are:
1.
2.
3.

Starting Cash:

☐ $5,000 ☐ $10,000 ☐ $20,000 ☐ $30,000 ☐ $50,000 ☐ $100,000 ☐ Unlimited

☐ Other: I will start with $_____ for this paper trading exercise.

Time frame:

☐ 1 month ☐ 3 months ☐ 6 months ☐ 1 year ☐ Unlimited

☐ Other: I will run this paper trading exercise for _____ months/years.

Screens: (You can screen potential stocks by price, the market they trade upon, the industry they are involved in, or any other parameters you think will help you achieve your goals).

☐ NASDAQ Stocks Only ☐ Shares Under $2 Only ☐ Only Biotech Stocks ☐ Only IPO's

☐ No Technology Stocks ☐ Only Technology Stocks

☐ Only Companies with Earnings

☐ Other: For this paper trading exercise, I will limit my pool of stocks using the following screens; _____, _____, _____,
_____.

Transaction Prices of Record:

☐ Close of Trading Each Day ☐ Open of Trading Each Day ☐ Price of Stocks When I Decide to Make the Paper Trade ☐ High Price for The Day ☐ Low Price for The Day

☐ Average Price for The Day

☐ Other: I will use _____ as my recorded prices for buy and sell transactions.

Brokerage Commissions:

☐ No Commissions (Free Trading) ☐ $10 per Buy/Sell ☐ $20 per Buy/Sell ☐ 1% of the Value of the Transaction

Additional Comments:

Differences between paper trading and real trading:

When you make the jump to trading real money, you may suddenly find that your stocks are not performing as you had anticipated. There are several reasons that may cause this situation.

1. **Your emotions take over.** While you may have been careless and aggressive with imaginary money, your decisions and thought processes will be different once you start using your hard-earned dollars. Paper traders are generally immune to greed, panic, anger, and impatience until they dive in with real money.

2. **Market activity will be different** from the time you tried out a paper trading strategy until you start trading actual stocks. While paper trading, the markets may have held up well, only to crash once you put a few dollars in. Always compare your trading results to the overall markets.

3. **The rules will be different**, especially if you used something like the daily closing price to record your transaction levels. In real life, you can not buy or sell a stock 'at the closing price,' but instead are subject to intraday volumes and activity. You may even see yourself getting partial fills, such as 1,000 of the 5,000 shares you wanted, because the volume was not great enough at your limit price.

Note! There is an excellent online tool that allows you to paper trade with real stocks in real time. Go to www.Investopedia.com and sign up for their trading simulator. It will really help put the fun into paper trading!

Chapter Two:
Trading Stocks

Trading stocks is quite simple, and it is not any different whether you are dealing with penny stocks or other equities.

Trading Penny Stocks Simplified

Yes, you can go online to your broker and click 'buy these shares, sell those,' and you're done. You do not need to know all the concepts below, but I strongly suggest learning them so that next time you click 'buy these shares' and you wind up paying more than you expected, or you don't get all the shares you wanted, you will know exactly why.

In the simplest form, it is a breeze to buy or sell a stock.

The first thing you need is a broker. There is much more about getting a good stock broker in upcoming sections of *Understanding Penny Stocks*. Simply put, they buy and sell for you based on your instructions, and take a small commission for their troubles.

Let's say you are interested in shares of ABC Corporation. Let's also assume that the ticker symbol (more about this later) is ABCD, the stock last traded at 45 cents, and you want to put about $500 into it. You think the price will go up over time, and decide you want to buy.

You go online to your brokerage account, enter that you want to buy 1,000 shares of ABCD, and click 'submit.' That's it! You've bought a stock.

Your brokerage account will reflect 1,000 shares of ABCD. If the price was still 45 cents when you bought, $450 will be taken from the cash in your broker account to cover the purchase, plus a few dollars for their commission (usually around $15).

Perhaps the price of ABCD is 75 cents a few months later. You decide to take your profits. Click click click. Online, you submit a trade through your broker to sell 1,000 shares of ABCD. $750 (less a small broker commission) gets put into your account. You have made a $300 profit on top of your original $450, and now you have $750 to invest in whatever stock you have your eye on.

It really is that simple.

Of course, learning the mechanics of trading is the easy part. Learning the art of trading is a bit more involved. In the next Chapter of *Understanding Penny Stocks* I reveal Leeds Analysis, which will help you uncover the really big penny stock gainers.

First, it is time to make a decision!

Option One - Keep it Simple: If you are comfortable with the simplified version of trading I provided above, and are ready to get into more specific detail about buying and selling, then continue with the next section.

Option Two - Learn the Most: If you want to learn the inner workings of the stock exchanges and trade orders, keep reading below. The following information is not needed to trade and profit from penny stocks. However, it will help you make better and more profitable trades.

NOTE: I will throw a lot of terms at you in this section (bid, ask, volume...) but understand that I am intentionally over-complicating the issue.

All the items I refer to (bid, ask, volume, etc...) are easily pulled up for any stock, through your broker or most free, online quote services.

In the most basic sense, a bunch of people trying to buy shares are matched up with a bunch of people trying to sell shares of the same company, and whenever a price is agreed upon, a trade takes place.

In other words, you are simply spending money to buy a stock, or selling a stock to get the money. Once you have a broker, you just give them your trade orders, and they worry about matching it up with other orders at the market.

In the following discussion we will use ABC Corp. as our stock. ABC is a fictional company just for the purposes of my explanation.

Starting from the Very, Very Beginning:

Stocks represent ownership in the underlying company.

If there are 1 million shares trading, 1 share usually is representative of 1 millionth of the company's value. The price of that share will change partially, but not entirely, based on the perceived value of the company (which changes over time).

As a company grows in size and brings in more money, the shares will generally increase in price. You may have owned 1 millionth of a company worth $1 million, but later that share could be 1 millionth of a company worth $7 million. Technically, your share should now be trading at $7. However, your shares may have increased 7 times over or 3 times over, or 20 times over.

Of course, there are thousands of other factors that may alter the value of the stock, but I will not be delving into them at this point, so I can keep my explanation simple.

Stock exchanges provide a service where they match up buyers and sellers of securities. They pool all the people trying to sell a specific stock into one group, and pool all those trying to buy the same stock into another.

Exchanges operate on price priority. Of all the potential buyers, the one willing to pay (bid) the most is at the front of the line. Of all the sellers, the one willing to sell (ask) their shares for the lowest price is also at the front of the line.

How a Stock's Price Changes:

A Change in Fundamentals:

If a company suddenly comes out with some good news, people may be willing to pay more for shares. They will raise their bid prices. At the same time, however, the sellers may realize that their shares are worth more due to the company's recent announcement, and therefore raise their asking prices.

A Change in Technicals:

Supply and demand can affect share prices to a great degree. For example, investors buying shares may outnumber those selling at any given point, and the lack of supply and strong demand may combine to drive up prices.

Now that you have learned all this, just forget it! That's right. You do not need to know all the inner workings of the stock market or how a trade takes place in order to make money trading penny stocks. You do not need to know how an engine works to be able to drive a car.

What you do need to know about trading stocks starts right here:

Bid: The amount a trader is willing to pay for shares of a company.

Ask: The amount at which a shareholder is willing to sell shares of a company.

Stock exchanges take the highest price being bid and the lowest price being asked. If these agree, or overlap (i.e. - best bid/buy price is $1.15, best ask/sell is $1.15) a trade will take place. In this example, shares will trade at $1.15.

Exchanges continually fulfill all the trades until the highest price someone is willing to pay (the bid) does not meet the lowest price at which someone is willing to sell (the ask). (For example, highest bid is $0.45 and the lowest ask is $0.55). At that point, no more trades will take place until someone raises their bid or lowers their ask. In other words, buyers and sellers are differing in their opinion of the value of the underlying shares, and until they agree nothing happens.

Here is an Example of How Trade Orders for ABC Corp. Could Stack Up:						
Buyers of ABC			**Sellers of ABC**			
Investor A: Bid 5,000 shares at $0.45	Investor B: Bid 1,000 shares at $0.48	Investor C: Bid 7,000 shares at $0.50	Investor W: Ask 3,000 shares at $0.55	Investor X: Ask 10,000 shares at $0.59	Investor Y: Ask 3,000 shares at $0.59	Investor Z: Ask 2,000 shares at $0.70

Some Examples:

In the above scenario, consider the following examples of what might happen:

• If none of these investors changed their bids, and no new investors entered orders, no shares would trade. In the above example, there is no agreement between buyers and sellers. The most anyone will pay is 50 cents, but the least anyone will sell for is 55 cents.

• Investor B raises his bid to $0.55. Investor B would get 1,000 shares at $0.55, while investor W sells 1,000 at $0.55, and still has an order standing to sell the remaining 2,000 at that price.

• Or, let's say that Investor X does not want to wait any more. She changes her order from a "limit order" (where she dictates the price), to a "market order" (where she gets the best available prices immediately). She would instantly end up selling 7,000 shares to investor C at $0.50, as well as 1,000 shares to Investor B at $0.48, and finally the last 2,000 to investor A at $0.45.

• What if a new investor comes along? (let's call him Investor D) He wants to buy 4,000 shares at $0.54. He instantly goes to the front of the buyer's line, ahead of investors A, B, and C, because he has the highest bid price. Yet, he still does not get any shares, because no one is willing to sell for less than 55 cents.

There are Two Types of Orders You Can Use to Trade Stocks:

Market Order:

You want to trade shares of a stock, and are willing to pay whatever the best available price is. You will be assured that you will get the stock, but you have no guarantee of the price you pay.

Limit Order:

You want to trade shares, but are only willing to make that trade at a certain price per share. For limit orders you need to set a price limit.

Market Orders versus Limit Orders For simplicity of explanation, I will pretend you are buying shares. The following points apply to selling as well, but in reverse.	
Market Orders	**Limit Orders**
You will take the best available price	You will only buy at the price you stipulate, or one that is even better for you
You do not need to specify a price or a time when the order will expire	You must specify the price you are willing to pay, and the date at which your order expires if it is not filled
You instantly get your shares	No trade will take place if there are not sufficient shares being sold at the price you stipulated
You will get all the shares you wanted	You may get a "partial fill" (meaning that you only get some of the shares you wanted) if there were some, but not enough shares for sale at the price you picked
You may end up paying more per share than you had wanted, especially if your buy order is large, or the underlying stock is subject to low trading volume	You control the price, and protect yourself from unexpected volatility

I highly discourage the use of market orders, especially with penny stocks	I always recommend using limit orders with penny stocks

Remember, I am intentionally over-complicating the issue of trading stocks for the purposes of education. This discussion makes trading stocks sound far more difficult than it really is. You can simply tell your broker to, "buy this," and "sell that," and it is not necessary to understand what all the other traders are doing.

Some Market Order Examples:

If you are buying with a market order, you will get the least expensive shares available. This also guarantees that you will get the shares you want, but there is a problem with market orders. Since you can not dictate the price you are willing to pay per share, you will be subject to price volatility.

What does that mean? Picture this scenario:

• You want to buy 4,000 shares of ABC, so you put in a market order.
• There are 1,000 shares for sale at $1.10, then 6,000 at $1.85.
• Your market order would instantly get you 1,000 shares at $1.10, and the remaining 3,000 at $1.85.

When you see how much you paid, you may be surprised, especially since you had seen that the lowest asking price had been $1.10.

Another scenario: What if someone else put in a market order seconds before you, and gobbled up all the lower-priced shares? You may find that you get all 4,000 shares at $1.85.

Consider another example just to make sure I am explaining it well enough:

• You want to buy 5,000 shares of ABC at the market price.

• You know that 2,000 shares are available at $0.75 because of your latest stock quote, so you enter the order.

• Let's assume that the next best asking price may be 1,000 shares at $0.95, then 10,000 shares at $1.15.

• Your 5,000 share market order would have yielded 2,000 shares at $0.75, 1,000 at $0.95, and the remaining 2,000 at $1.15.

This would leave the current asking price of ABC at 8,000 shares at $1.15, while the bid would probably remain wherever it was before you came along.

Market orders can be dangerous with penny stocks due to their low trading volume, as discussed above.

A Limit Order Example:

You want to trade shares, but are only willing to authorize the trade at a certain price, or one that is even better for you.

For example, you want to buy 5,000 of ABC at $0.80 or less. Given the above example (ask prices = 2,000 shares @ 75 cents, 1,000 @ 95 cents, 10,000 shares @ $1.15), you would yield 2,000 shares at $0.75 and that is where the trading would end. 3,000 shares would go unfilled unless someone offered to sell at $0.80 or less during the duration of your order.

One Stand-Alone Example: Buying Shares	
Best Bid Price:	Best Ask Price:
6,000 shares of ABC being bid at $1.05	4,000 shares of ABC for sale at $1.20

Let's assume you want to buy 2,000 shares of ABC. Here are some examples of how you could proceed:

• Use a market order (I discourage this). You would get 2,000 shares at $1.20 (unless something changed in the time it took you to place your order with your broker).

• You could put in a limit order at $1.06 or higher. This would put you first in priority sequence of buyers, until someone else out-bid you. As long as you are first in line, if anyone sells shares it will need to be to you. You may have to wait, and you may not get any shares if no one decides to sell at that price.

• You could put in a limit order at $1.05 (you would be second in line behind the original $1.05 buy order). Or you could even bid lower (you would be behind everyone with a higher bid price, and would not get shares until their orders were filled, and only IF prices of ABC came down to your bid price. You could make the order good for a few days/weeks, and hope that shares would eventually dip to meet your bid.

• If you really wanted the shares, and thought that $1.20 was a good price, I would suggest doing the following: put in a limit order at $1.25. You would get your 2,000 shares at $1.20 if that sell order was still active by the time your order hit the trading floor. No matter what, you would never pay more than $1.25, even if the lowest asking price was $2.50. Use limit orders whenever you can, even when you are willing to pay more than the current asking price. (Traders using market orders often end up paying way more than they had intended).

OK, enough complicated stuff. It just gets easy from here on out.

Chapter Two:
Buying Penny Stocks

Two Ways to Enter Your Trades: Computer or Telephone

So, you have decided that you want to buy some shares of ABC. You need to know the following details for your order to proceed:

1. The ticker symbol of the stock.

(In this case, ABC). You may also need to know the name of the company, which is ABC Corporation for the purposes of our example.

2. The market which the stock is trading on.

In our example, we will say that ABC trades on the AMEX.

3. The number of shares you want to buy.

This is referred to as 'volume' of shares. We will say that you have $3,500 in available cash in your trading account, but only want to spend about $1,500 on this stock. The most recent trading price was around $0.50 per share.

Thus, you would probably want to order 3,000 shares (which would total $1,500 before commissions, assuming you bought at $0.50).

4. Market or Limit price?

Be sure to review my full description of the types of trade orders, earlier in this book.

If you choose market, you do not know what price you will pay for shares, but you will be assured that the trade will go through.

Alternatively, you can set a limit price. I will say $0.60 for our example, meaning that you will pay $0.60 or less for each share.

If there is insufficient selling below that price you may wind up getting none or only a fraction of the shares you wanted. You feel that ABC has good daily trading volume, and since your order is small, and your limit price is a 20% premium to the last traded price, you feel confident that your order will be filled.

As well, when you got a recent quote on ABC you saw that there were 9.0 lots for sale at $0.50, which equals 9,000 shares currently being offered at $0.50.

In that scenario, your limit order to buy 3,000 shares at $0.60 would result in a purchase of 3,000 shares at $0.50.

5. Decide on the duration of your order.

Market orders do not require a duration, because since you are willing to take the best available price, your order will be instantly filled when it hits the trading floor.

Limit orders do require a duration, and you will get an additional brokerage commission every day that a part of that order gets filled. To buy 3,000 ABC over 3 days (assuming you only got 1,000 each day at your limit price) would triple your total commission cost. You decide that you want to guarantee to only pay one commission, so you make the order good for the day. This is called a 'day order.' You can also choose to keep the order open for days or weeks at a time.

6. Total Cost

Know the total costs you would have to pay. Take into account commissions.

You are now ready to enter your order to buy 3,000 ABC shares on the AMEX at $0.60, good for the day.

We highly recommend that if you have the option, do your very first trade order on the phone with a live broker. Even though most brokerages will charge a slightly higher commission for this service, they will catch any errors you might have made, and can answer any questions. As well, some brokers will even be able to tell you if your order was filled (for market orders only) while you wait right there on the phone.

Tell them that it is your first order, and they will most likely be extra helpful.

Open Order:

Until your order expires (at the end of the duration you have set), or is filled (3,000 shares of ABC have been bought), your order is considered 'open.'

Monitor your open orders. You should be able to check these quite easily if you have an online brokerage account. Watch to see how many shares you have gotten and what price you paid.

If at the end of the trading day you have acquired 2,500 of 3,000 shares, and your order was good for two days, you may want to cancel the rest of the 500 that the order calls for. This will help you avoid paying a second commission, in case the other 500 would get bought the next day.

Order Checklist: Buying Shares

Ticker Symbol of the Stock: _____

Company Name: (probably not required) _____

Buying or Selling: (In this example you are buying shares, so check 'buying')

☐ Buying   ☐ Selling

Market the Stock Trades On:

☐ NASDAQ SmallCap   ☐ OTC-BB   ☐ Pink Sheets   ☐ Over-The-Counter

☐ Other: ABC Corp. trades on the _____.

Volume:

I want to buy _____ thousand shares. (You can also buy by the hundred, or in odd lots (ie-53 shares, 1 share, 98 shares...) but that may cost you a special commission from your broker)

Order Type:

☐ Market Order   ☐ Limit Order

Market orders will be filled instantly, but you can not be sure of the price you will pay per share	For limit orders you will need to know: Your limit price per share: _____ When will the order expire: ☐ Good till close (day order, expires when markets close at 4pm Eastern Standard Time) ☐ Other: I want my order to remain active until the end of the day on: _____.

Chapter Two:
Selling Penny Stocks

Selling is almost entirely the same process as buying. You will need to know the same 6 points:

1. The ticker symbol of the stock.

2. The market which the stock is trading on.

3. The number of shares you want to sell.

4. Market or Limit price?

5. Decide on the duration of your order.

6. Know the total costs you would have to pay, including commissions.

Pretend that ABC exploded in price while you held 3,000 shares, and hit $2.95. You want to take your profits from 2,000 shares and let the remaining 1,000 ride. You would contact your broker online or by phone, with the following information:

Selling 2,000 shares of ABC (on AMEX) at $2.90, good through Friday the 11th.

One Scenario: Perhaps your first 1,000 would sell at $2.95. Then you still have 1,000 shares in your open order, and you see that the best bid is $2.75. You could either wait it out (your order is going to stay active until the end of trading on Friday, the 11th), or lower your asking price (see 'changing open orders' in the upcoming section).

You decide to drop your asking price to $2.75. In this case, the next 1,000 shares would almost certainly sell. You would get $2.75 per share for this second block of 1,000.

You have now brought in $2,950 from the first block of 1,000 shares, $2,750 from the next block, and you still hold 1,000 shares in your account. You will have the $5,700 deposited into your account, less the commissions your broker charges.

It is simple stuff, and once you have made one or two trades, you will realize how easy it really is!

In upcoming sections, I show you the **Top Brokers for Penny Stock Traders**, how to monitor and change your trade orders on the fly, and how to pick penny stocks that are about to explode in price. So, let's get to it!

Chapter Two:
Changing or Canceling Open Trade Orders

You may change your mind on an open order and cancel it.

This is quite simple to do (contact your broker for details) but you will be responsible for prior fills. In other words, if 1,000 shares traded from your account in the time before you cancelled, this part of the trade is irreversible.

Changing orders is also an easy task, and the details will differ depending on your broker. You are still responsible for prior fills and you can not change the stock in question, or the volume. (If you want to change the stock or the volume, just cancel the one order and make an entirely new one).

There are facets of a trade order you can change. You will be able to change the order from a limit order to a market order, adjust your price, or alter your duration.

Chapter Two:
Monitoring Your Stocks and Trade Orders

You should always keep a close eye on your trading account to verify not only that your orders went through, but that there is no discrepancy in the price of shares, volume, or details of the transaction.

Once you have some shares, or even if you just want to watch those stocks you are interested in before you buy them, you should spend as much time as possible checking into the fundamentals and trading activity of the equities.

I reveal the most widely recognized and effective method for picking penny stocks, called Leeds Analysis, in the next chapter.

There is a direct correlation between research and returns.

When monitoring your stocks and trade orders, you may spot warning signs, or uncover an excellent buying opportunity.

You will find that the Internet is an excellent source of data and information, and there are many different tools available. As well there are a number of offline sources, and we provide a comprehensive look at many of them, online and offline, in Chapter Seven on Information Sources.

Of course, you are probably excited to begin trading right away. First, you will need to decide on a discount broker, which is what I discuss in the next section.

If you already have a broker that you are happy with, and that can trade penny stocks, you may want to skip ahead to the really good stuff.

Chapter Two:
Getting a Good Stock Broker

NOTE: See below for my Top Broker Rankings!

Getting a trading account set up is as simple as opening a bank account. For most online discount brokers, you can do the whole process over the Internet.

There are Two Types of Brokers:

Discount:

I strongly recommend using a discount broker. Usually you can open an online trading account, which is certainly the best way to go to monitor and view all your trades, history of transactions, and to get quotes and information on the stocks that interest you.

They are also less expensive, often allowing trades for as little as $5.

Full Service:

These deal one on one with the client, and are usually better suited for traders with very large portfolios. The commissions are high, usually several hundred dollars for the same trade you could have made for $15 through a discount broker.

You will have access to a full service broker's advice, and they will come to you with investment ideas. They are generally afraid of penny stocks and discourage their clients from investing in such equities.

Choosing a Broker:

First you need to decide on your own requirements from your broker. There are many choices out there competing for you as a client, so be choosy and make sure to get the best one for your own needs.

Perhaps you are not starting with a large amount of money, and therefore high commissions will be too expensive. Will you be involved with foreign stocks, and do the brokers you have in mind have strict policies for foreign trading? Will you be trading bonds? Canadian stocks? Do you have an existing broker you are happy with? Do they allow penny stock trades? Will you only be able to trade by phone?

We feel the best approach is to have one good broker, not three or four. If you currently have several brokerage accounts, consider transferring all of your assets to the one broker who works best for you overall.

Broker Criteria:

Commissions:

I have found that this is the most important consideration for most penny stock traders, due to the higher trade frequency, and the lower total dollar amounts, which makes brokerage fees very significant. However, I also feel that this should not be the primary consideration, assuming that the brokers you like have competitive rates.

Speed of Order Execution:

I feel that this is the most overrated criterion when choosing a broker.

Despite what advertisements may lead you to believe, the speeds of most brokers are approximately the same.

While penny stocks can be volatile, they will usually sit within each price range more than long enough for you to enter and exit at the prices you decide. It will more likely be your own hesitation or the time it takes you to make your trading decisions that will affect your trading prices.

Reliability:

This can be very important. Brokers do make mistakes, and their web sites go down, and even their computerized trading programs can foul up. There is nothing more annoying than going to make a time-sensitive trade and being unable to access the web site.

Policies:

This is the most important consideration for penny stock investors in my opinion. Policies include things like the minimum required balance (if any), commissions on penny stocks and foreign stocks compared to regular fees, monthly fees, and the ability (or inability) to trade shares from the penny stock markets. While one broker may not allow trades in shares under $1.00, and requires a $2,000 minimum deposit, another may not have limitations on either.

Accessibility:

If a trade does go wrong, or even if you just have a quick question, you need to be able to get through to your broker without sitting on hold all day long. You also want to feel that your questions and concerns get answered, regardless of whether it is by e-mail, phone, or otherwise.

Customer Service:

On a similar note, when you do get through, are their replies professional and courteous? More importantly, are they timely and correct?

Research and Tools:

This should be a secondary consideration. There are so many free sources for data and information that you may not ever use the 'bell and whistle' features that your broker provides.

BROKER	Trading Direct	LowTrades	Scottrade	Ameritrade	E-Trade
OVERALL RANK	**1**	**2**	**3**	**4**	**5**
COMMISSION PRICE	1	1	4	3	5
RELIABILITY	1	3	2	4	5
CUSTOMER SATISFACTION	1	3	3	4	5
CONFLICT RESOLUTION	3	1	2	5	4
CUSTOMER SERVICE	3	2	1	4	5
SPEED OF EXECUTION	1	2	3	4	5
TOTAL SCORE (lower is better)	10	14	18	28	34

OUR CURRENT CHAMPION:

TradingDirect.com
TradingDirect has no minimum opening balance for an individual cash account. You will need to conduct at least one trade per year, or else you get a $60 inactivity charge.

Each on-line trade, limit or market is just $9.95. Penny stocks are not treated any differently than any other stock.

TradingDirect is very helpful by e-mail, and not bad by telephone either.

For penny stock traders, TradingDirect.com beat all the other brokers.

THE BEST OF THE REST:

Lowtrades.com

Lowtrades has made some much needed improvements to their website. They have an excellent investing overview section and offer free real time streaming quotes. Their customer service reps are also very knowledgeable and friendly. Fortunately, all of these upgrades haven't affected their incredibly low service fees.

There is no minimum opening balance for an individual cash account. Lowtrades does have a semi-annual inactivity fee of $30 but it is automatically waived if you conduct 1 trade every 6 months.

Each on-line trade, limit or market is just $5. If you conduct a trade over the phone, each transaction will cost you $25. Penny stocks are not treated any differently than any other stock.

With Lowtrades you can purchase companies listed on the Canadian exchanges but you need to conduct those transaction over the phone with one of their brokers. The commission fee for each Canadian transaction, like all broker-assisted trades, is $25.

Scottrade

A small brokerage firm with lower over-head and commissions, Scottrade has a beefed up website with a long list of products and services, including free real time streaming news from Dow Jones and free unlimited real time streaming quotes and charts. If conducting trades is your main priority - then Scottrade is a good choice. Unless of course you live in Canada; Scottrade is not registered to conduct business there.

With Scottrade, you need to have an opening balance of only $500, there is no yearly inactivity fee, and they do not charge account maintenance fees. On-line market trades on shares over $1.00 are only $7 and limit orders are $12. For broker assisted trades, market orders are $17 and limit orders are $22.

Scottrade will trade penny stocks, but they are conducted under different rules. All trades on stocks under $1.00 will cost you $12 plus 0.5% of the principle amount. For Pink Sheet and stocks traded in Canada you need to speak with a broker (they cannot be conducted on-line). For these, the commission fee is $22 per trade plus .5% of the principle amount.

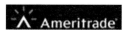

Ameritrade

Boasting the most on-line trades in the industry Ameritrade has an informative website with a vast array of trading tools and services. While you need a minimum of $500 to open a cash account, an opening balance of $1000 will get you 25 commission free on-line trades (limited time offer - good for the first 5 weeks).

There is a non-activity fee of $15 per quarter but it is waived if your minimum balance is $2000 or if you make more than 4 trades every six months.

All on-line trades are just $10.99; if you want to conduct a trade over their automated phone the service fee is $14.99. If you need to speak to a broker to conduct your trade, a market order is $24.99 and limit orders are $29.99.

Ameritrade allows for trades in penny stocks and the on-line commissions are the same as non penny stocks: $10.99.

E-Trade

e-Trade's minimum requirement to open a regular cash account is $1000. While there is no inactivity fee for the first year, e-Trade will start charging a quarterly fee of $25 beginning in the following year. That fee is waived though if you have conducted 2 or more trades in the previous 6 months or if you have an account balance of $5000.

All market and limit orders are $19.99, with an additional $3 service fee. That said the trade commission goes down to $9.99 on the 27th trade done in any given quarter.

If at any time you trade more than 5000 shares on the NYSE, you will be levied with a 1 cent per share charge...on top of commissions. If you decide you want to conduct a broker assisted trade, add $45 on top of everything else.

e-Trade does trade in stocks listed on the OTC-BB and Pink Sheets and the commission fees are the same as those mentioned above.

These are my broker rankings, but I can not know what criteria may be important for you personally. For this reason, if you are looking for a broker, I suggest reading the next section, on **Where to Research the Stock Brokers**.

If you are not looking for a broker, then you should probably skip ahead to the really good stuff.

Chapter Two:
Where to Research the Stock Brokers

Do not take your broker decision lightly. A bad broker may not only cost you time, money, or aggravation, but may spoil your entire trading experience.

You should trust word of mouth from people you know, and look into your own trading needs versus their policies. So where do you begin?

Just remember that what may be a good broker for one investor's needs may not necessarily be the best for another. The broker best suited to you depends on your preferences in terms of commission fees, service and support, reliability, speed of service, trading restrictions and other factors.

In other words, you need to come to your own decision based on your personal criteria.

Everyone's brokerage needs are different.

If you are in the market for a broker, you should consider visiting one of the many online brokerage-ranking web sites. There are several of them. It could save you a great deal of time and hassle, and most likely a good deal of money on commissions as well.

You may want to contact the brokerages, if not to have questions answered, then just to see their response times and accessibility.

Word of mouth is an excellent source. Keep in mind that your personal trading requirements may be different from those of your friend.

 **Waterhouse**

My personal word of mouth referral to you: TD Waterhouse. I have been trading for a long time, and they are the only broker I have ever used. That says something in itself, and I have had very few issues with them over hundreds of trades. They are also available online, or on the phone (automated or in person). While their commissions are higher than most, it is offset by their reliability, the security of being backed by a big bank (TD Canada Trust), and excellent accessibility.

Television and Media:

We discourage paying any attention to broker advertisements and marketing schemes. It is generally the big 'assembly line' brokers that have the most convincing, and most frequent advertisements. They are not well equipped to handle the volume of clients that their marketing and low commissions generate, and are hard pressed to offer competitive reliability, accountability, or accessibility.

Changing Brokers and Transferring Accounts:

This process is simpler than you may think. Inform your new broker of your intentions to move your account to them, and they will handle the rest. They will have you fill out the authorization form that allows them to move your assets from your old brokerage account into theirs. Approximately three days later you will find all of your shares and money in your new account.

Now we are finally ready to get to the really important stuff. In Chapter Three of *Understanding Penny Stocks*, I reveal how to discover winning penny stocks using Leeds Analysis, and how to get in early to ride them all the way up!

So, Let's Proceed!

Chapter Three:
How to Choose the Winners

The information you are about to discover has long been secret among a few industry insiders.

Years of work from experienced research specialists has culminated into what you are about to read. These concepts will enable you to uncover your own explosive penny stocks before they make their moves.

These concepts are best understood if approached in order, starting with Picking Your Own Explosive Penny Stocks.

Chapter Three:
Picking Your Own Explosive Penny Stocks

A little work can go a long way.

In the case of penny stocks, the amount of effort and research you put into finding the perfect investments is directly proportional to success.

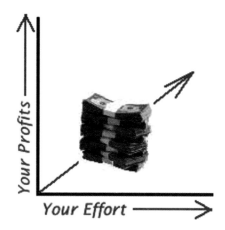

Almost all traders who get involved with penny stocks are doing so for the wrong reasons. For example, they hear a hot tip from a friend at work, or see a small news article about a company in the paper. Unfortunately, by the time you hear about the shares, they are already common knowledge.

This is not to say that you will need to research for eight hours a day just to make money. It is quite the opposite actually. A few moments of effort, along with the knowledge and concepts revealed in Leeds Analysis, will help you quickly identify which are the best penny stocks from the pool of thousands.

For those of you who are willing to research extensively, the theories will be incredibly valuable.

If you are not inclined to do very much work, or do not have the time to commit, these concepts become even more important. They will show you how to;

- Easily rank stocks
- Avoid the common mistakes

Perhaps you do not want to do any research yourself at all, but instead prefer to use the professional penny stock picking services offered by PeterLeeds.com. This is also an excellent way to proceed, because our results have proven reliable and accurate. By subscribing to my *Penny Stock Insider* newsletter, you will get all the penny stock picks you can handle.

A Little Work:

As I have mentioned, a little work can go a long way. However, most traders do not put in the required effort, or any effort for that matter. Those of you who are willing to do the extra due diligence or analysis will benefit greatly from what you are about to read.

Understand that 95% of penny stock companies should be considered bad or dangerous investments. However, the proven approach outlined in the next several sections of *Understanding Penny Stocks* makes it easy to tell which stocks should be ruled out.

A Long Way:

As you become more experienced, you will learn that a good penny stock trader can make money on good and bad penny stocks alike, simply by investing at the right time. Since every stock fluctuates, you shall see that **money can be made by buying even the worst companies at the right time, and money can be lost by buying the best companies at the wrong time.**

Ideally you want to accumulate the best penny stock companies at the most advantageous prices. We suggest using fundamental analysis (detailed in an upcoming section) to discover which are the best penny stock companies, while using technical analysis (also detailed later) to pick the most opportune buying prices.

Chapter Three:
Different Research and Analysis Schools of Thought

There are many different strategies for picking winning stocks, and perhaps you have heard of most of them.

From 'advanced technical analysis trading programs' to 'computer-assisted undervalued screens,' no one method has consistently proven effective with penny stocks.

You may as well have been throwing darts at the stock page in the newspaper!

For this reason, my company has developed our own proprietary research and analysis technique **which applies specifically to the penny stock markets**. Our methodology has been working exceptionally well, and has been fine-tuned over many years to further increase its effectiveness.

You are about to learn this long-secretive approach to picking winning penny stocks, called Leeds Analysis. This technique has helped me make tremendous amounts of money, both for myself and for my subscribers of *Penny Stock Insider*.

However, I first ask that you review the different research and analysis schools of thought. I believe that it is very important to understand the numerous ways that investors have attempted to beat the market over time. The roots of my own secretive penny stock research and analysis technique stems from some of the best pieces of the following methodologies.

I feel that I must make one thing clear! The methodologies presented below were created to apply to higher priced equities, and when applied to penny stocks they often lose their relevance and accuracy. That is why myself and my team were forced to create our own approach to picking penny stocks, which is detailed in the next section of *Understanding Penny Stocks*.

Why don't conventional research techniques work for penny stocks, you ask?

This is because penny stocks are an animal all their own, and they play by significantly different rules. When investors try to take a strategy for investing and apply it to penny stocks, they are often surprised by how ineffective it can be.

The Different Schools of Thought:

Technical Analysis:

This uses patterns in the trading chart to try to uncover trends, and then predict the future direction of shares. It is also done in an attempt to uncover the best buying and selling opportunities and prices, as well as to predict the future activity of the underlying stock.

For example, when most stocks demonstrate what TA calls a 'cup and handle' pattern, they generally spike higher in the subsequent weeks. Thus, a cup and handle pattern may be a good buying opportunity.

TA is significantly limited when applied to penny stocks, as the trading volumes and low investor interest (compared to most stocks) negates most analysis patterns. TA works best on well-followed, heavy volume shares like IBM or FORD.

"Conventional" TA can not and should not be applied to penny stocks. Instead, we have developed our own TA methodology for application specifically to penny stocks, and I detail it in upcoming sections of *Understanding Penny Stocks*.

Fundamental Analysis:

This approach uses the company's financial statements. It looks at the financial numbers and ratios, as well as the corporate situation. We feel that fundamental analysis is a great starting point for screening and researching penny stocks, and that it is an effective method of finding the best companies to invest in.

Fundamental analysis looks at things from revenues and debt, to ratios like price/earnings and debt/equity. It then compares these with other stocks in general, and with direct competitors. Using fundamental analysis, you will also look at such criteria as management team effectiveness, press releases, brand recognition, barriers to entry for new competitors to the sector, among a host of other parameters.

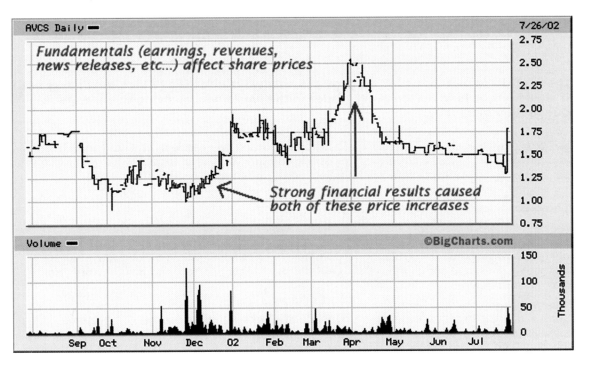

Fundamental analysis is an excellent way to research and rank stocks. However, it becomes more difficult when dealing with penny stocks since it is often challenging to get access to all of the required information (and even when you do, you often need to be wary of the reliability of the facts).

Later, in the section on Information Sources, I detail how you can go about finding the information you need. In the next section, I explain to you exactly what fundamental factors drive the share prices of penny stocks based on our research.

Individual Concepts:

The pure depth of fundamental analysis can be daunting, and as a result many trading concepts have sprung up from FA roots to take on lives of their own.

For example, some research methods simply take one fundamental concept such as price/earnings ratio, and use that as a way to compare investments. The companies with the lowest P/E ratios would be considered undervalued, while the ones with the highest P/E ratios would be overvalued. (One flaw with the approach in this example is that it assumes that all other factors are equal).

Another may look just at insider trading. When insiders are buying, it must be a good time to load up on shares, and when they are selling, they must be privy to some bad news. (Insiders are just people, though, and often they can sell shares to raise money for their daughter's braces or a new car. Other insiders 'go down with the ship' and never sell their shares while the company sinks. In other examples, there may not be enough clear insider activity to reveal anything at all).

If you are sensing a trend here, it is that these 'Individual Concept' investment approaches are easily flawed. Most are fads that may have worked on certain stocks in certain market environments, but they quickly become exposed as ineffective once they are applied by individual investors. While traders may get lucky in some markets, then swear by the effectiveness of the approach, all of these strategies have proven to be inconsistent over the long term.

If any of these methods ever did prove to be always effective (which they never will) it would not be long before every trader in the world was applying them, especially due to their simplicity.

Besides, why look at only one factor of a company, when you can look at all of them? True, you may be able to make some profits some of the time by seeing a small part of the picture, but revealing the entire picture will help you make more money, more of the time.

Themes:

You may have heard of some of them: undervalued stocks, bottom-fishing, industry leaders, rolling stocks, momentum investing (the last of which is a spin-off from technical analysis methods). These are sometimes effective if the market cooperates, and painful when the market misbehaves.

Sure, it is great to pick up shares in undervalued stocks when the market has bottomed out and has just begun to rebound. But in that sort of a market, is it not also a great idea to be involved with bottom-fishing, industry leaders, momentum investing, stocks that begin with the letter 'D', and investment horoscopes?

Look at January to March of the year 2000. The three months leading up to the bursting of the dot-com bubble, you could not have lost money in the market if you tried! (If you did, please write to me and tell me all about it. I would LOVE to hear how you pulled that off!)

Perhaps I am being a little harsh. Sometimes these methods listed above can help you uncover some good shares. Just beware of their gimmicks, and only get involved when the market is just right. As well, know that there is no substitute to getting the entire company picture, as I detail in the next section.

The method I am about to explain to you has consistently outperformed the market.

Think of this weight loss analogy: there are a thousand different gimmick diets you could try, and although you may see some temporary results (which do not last), they do not work. The best way to lose weight is through changing your eating habits and lifestyle. In other words, doing the work required rather than going with a gimmick. Similarly, the best way to make money in penny stocks is to do the work required, rather than going with a gimmick.

I believe penny stock traders (even those that use our professional penny stock picking service) should examine the fundamentals as described in the next section on Leeds Analysis. This will help you to discover the best penny stock companies, and find the best buying and selling prices at which to trade those shares.

Different Analysis Approaches		Why They Can Not Apply to Penny Stocks
Technical Analysis:	Using trading charts and activity to attempt to predict future trends and prices	TA requires high trading volumes and predictability of stock activity, neither of which are common enough with the majority of penny stocks.
Fundamental Analysis:	Using the financial results, assets, and earnings to predict the value of a company's shares.	Fundamental Analysis can be effective for penny stocks, **IF** it is applied with special considerations in mind. The fundamentals which drive the price of a blue-chip company are very different than those which drive a penny stock company, as detailed in Leeds Analysis.
Individual Concepts: P/E comparisons, momentum investing, revenue growth comparisons, and dozens of other solo theories.	Comparing companies by one factor (ie-Price/Earnings Ratio).	This method is too shallow even for large-cap and blue-chip stocks, and is even less effective for penny stocks, which are a much more complicated beast.
Themes: Rolling Stocks, Bottom-Fishing, Trend Trading, and other faulty 'quick fixes.'	Like fad-diets that don't work, theme-based stock picking is very marketable, but not very effective.	Like Individual Concepts mentioned above, Theme-Based techniques do not work to begin with, and have little chance of success when applied to the penny stock markets.

Chapter Three:
Leeds Analysis (Overview)

Here are full details of my long-hidden penny stock analysis techniques.

Recently these were not available to anyone, at any price. Now they are yours to browse, learn, and share with others.

The techniques in the following sections of *Understanding Penny Stocks* have been effectively used to generate thousands upon thousands of dollars in returns, and were instrumental in my uncovering many big-gainers, like DCSR which went from $0.46 to $10.00, and USNA which went from $1.55 to over $50 per share.

The Three Steps of Leeds Analysis

Step 1: Find Your Target

You can apply Leeds Analysis to a single stock to discover its quality, or to a group of stocks to find the best investment out of the bunch.

Step 2: Apply Fundamental Analysis

Fundamental analysis, as described in the upcoming sections, will reveal which are the best (and worst) companies, and the relative strength and potential of each.

Step 3: Apply Technical Analysis

Once you have uncovered the strongest companies, Technical Analysis will help you discover the best prices at which to buy and sell their shares.

Note: Don't know of any stocks to apply Leeds Analysis to? It's easy to get a short-list by using a stock screener. (See chapter 7)

Leeds Analysis Simplified:

It is much easier than it may first appear.

It is just like doing a house inspection. You look at every room, the pipes, the basement, the cupboards, the electrical system, and even the neighborhood and the neighbors! Do this for five or ten or twenty houses, and by the end you will know which are the best and the worst options.

If any house has even a single warning sign, such as a leaking roof, or an obnoxious neighbor, cross it off your list.

Doing the research is the hard part, and it is not even that hard. (Actually, I think it is quite fun). If you do this part properly, you won't even need to make a conscious decision on which penny stock is the best value for your money. You will automatically know. Usually, the answer becomes obvious when you are about two-thirds of the way through your Leeds Analysis.

Here is How Leeds Analysis Works:

- The prices of penny stocks are driven by certain criteria.
- Leeds Analysis guides you through all of those criteria, one at a time.
- By considering all factors, you will have a clear picture of the best penny stocks.

Things to Keep in Mind as You Proceed:

- This approach is a 'criteria based' system, meaning that each stock should be analyzed on each of the following parameters. This will be effective in eliminating poor investments, screening a long list down to the best prospects, or uncovering that one single stock which could change your life.

- While you are reviewing this methodology, keep in mind that a great penny stock does not have to enjoy outstanding marks in ALL of the following criteria, but the more the better.

- Also be aware that while it takes a handful of strong fundamentals to drive a penny stock higher, it often only takes one negative parameter to send it lower.

- Finally, a penny stock that you find which boasts excellent marks in most or all categories listed below is not necessarily a good investment AT THE CURRENT PRICE. You should follow up your fundamental analysis with our proprietary technical analysis techniques, (which are detailed in **Part Six to Part Ten** of Leeds Analysis) to pinpoint the best buying and selling opportunities.

Leeds Analysis Cheatsheet	
Fundamentals: To uncover the health, quality, and potential of a company	**Technicals:** To learn the best buy and sell prices for the stock
Primary: • Increasing Revenues • Improving Earnings • Competitive Advantages • Low Debt Levels • Insider Trades • Buy-Back Plans • Industry Conditions • Institutional Holdings • Political/Social Shifts • News and Press Releases • Alliances • Improving Financial Ratios Secondary: • Market Risk • Industry Risk • Legal Action / Law Suits • Competition • Management / Board Changes	• Dips • Collapse • Temporary Spike • Permanent Spike • Support Levels • Resistance Levels • General Range • Current Trend • Trend Reversal • Topping Out • Bottoming Out • Consolidation

Chapter Three:
Leeds Analysis - Fundamentals

Fundamental Parameters:

Much of the information you will need to accurately research the companies is included in their financial statements and annual reports. Much of this data is available online for free. I tell you more about finding this later, in **My Picks for Quality Websites**.

So what are you looking for, exactly? All of the following criteria can have an impact on the activity of the underlying shares and the success of the company. You can uncover the required information for each simply enough, and once you have done your analysis factor by factor, the big picture for any stock will seem as clear as day.

Leeds Analysis is really quite simple, and once you have learned to apply it to one stock, you'll know how to apply it to ten thousand.

The Parameters:

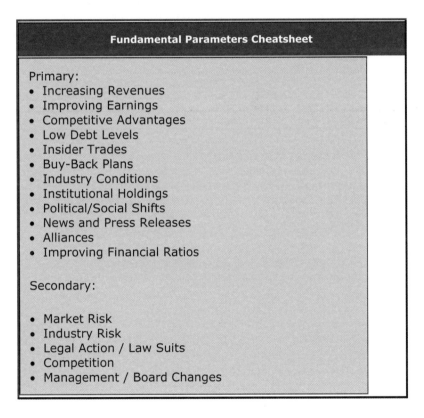

Fundamental Parameters Cheatsheet

Primary:
- Increasing Revenues
- Improving Earnings
- Competitive Advantages
- Low Debt Levels
- Insider Trades
- Buy-Back Plans
- Industry Conditions
- Institutional Holdings
- Political/Social Shifts
- News and Press Releases
- Alliances
- Improving Financial Ratios

Secondary:

- Market Risk
- Industry Risk
- Legal Action / Law Suits
- Competition
- Management / Board Changes

Increasing Revenues:

Of course, the more money a company is bringing in, the better.

However, I would also like to present the importance of this concept from another perspective. Companies that are enjoying improving revenues quarter over quarter, and year over year, do not need to increase their operational costs at the same growth rate.

For example, doubling of the number of faxes a company receives in a day does not mean they need to double the number of fax machines on hand. You see, most companies increase their expenses at a much slower rate than their revenues are rising. They enjoy better use of their infrastructure (machinery and staff and factories and company jets) to capture greater revenues, and thus get more value out of the existing situation they have in place. The end result is greater earnings.

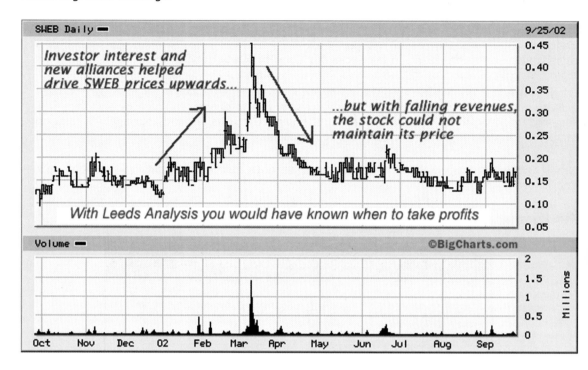

What is a good sign: A company that has enjoyed a consistent trend in revenue growth on a quarter by quarter basis. This may indicate that they are gaining market share, or that their operational strategy is proving out. This is especially true for companies that are building a subscriber base of clients that are subject to recurring billing. For example, a fiber-optic Internet provider that keeps previous clientele, while adding new ones to the monthly billing list will not only enjoy the increase in revenues, but will be able to sustain those levels.

What is a bad sign: A company that has expenses increasing in line with revenue growth may be doing something wrong. Also, decreasing revenues are a major danger sign for any company.

Improving Earnings:

Companies are in business to make money, end of story. Over time we have distorted that fact, and things have gotten very complicated with mergers and analyst coverage and lines of credit. Some corporations think it is acceptable to lose money, because they are "battling for market share."

In the end, a company can only survive by making more money than it spends. This is a fact, and a very painful one for many investors and corporations who have lost sight of the rules of the game.

Earnings are a measure of how much a company makes above what it spends to operate. If there were one most important fundamental aspect of a company (in reality there are dozens, but just if...) it would be earnings.

After all is said and done, and stock offerings are factored in, and restructuring charges, and currency exchange gains, and one-time charges, and a whole host of other items that you do not need to trouble yourself with right now, how much did a company make? When the smoke clears, you are looking at earnings.

Ignore EBITDA (earnings before interest, taxes, deductions and amortization) and ignore gross earnings. If you do not know what these are, it doesn't matter - you are ignoring them.

Only look at net earnings. While most companies are losing money, which is the case for about 85% of penny stocks, those that are bringing in more than they spend will be able to provide the total amount they made (ie- $1,934,023 for the three month period of February to May) as well as a per share amount (ie- $0.21 per share).

The latter number, earnings per share, is generally more useful. It can be compared to the current share price easily, and it puts all companies on a level playing field for comparison purposes. It ignores factors like the total amount of shares outstanding, which varies from one stock to the next, so your comparison between several companies will be more telling.

What is a good sign: Positive earnings immediately put a penny stock company above 85% of the others. If those earnings are showing signs of increasing from one quarter to the next, you may be able to profit greatly from the underlying shares, especially if you get in early and the trend of increasing earnings continues.

What is a bad sign: Negative earnings, although in some cases profit can be made trading companies that are losing money, if you buy into their shares at the right price.

As well, decreasing earnings over time may drive a company into the ground if they can not reverse the trend before they start taking losses.

Competitive Advantages:

Some companies do not compete on a level playing field. These are the penny stocks that you should want to invest in. I am not referring to temporary advantages that can be easily replicated. Look for those corporations who have a claim to their advantage, and will be able to leverage it for years or decades.

For example, one of the penny stocks I once picked for my subscribers was Silverline Technologies (SLT), which was a programming company for high-end computer applications. Their competitive advantage was that they were based in India, and it was almost laughable how inexpensively they could produce a quality program when compared to their U.S. based counterparts. They had an office in the U.S., and they programmed mostly for major U.S. companies. Their work was as good, and in most cases better than their competition, and there was no way that the domestic American corporations could match their price.

What is a good sign: The advantage is sustainable and not easily replicated. (See my SLT example above).

What is a bad sign: Companies that are lacking in a competitive advantage that their competitors all share. For example, if you were a publishing house, but you were not located in New York where most of your competitors and literary agents were based, it would be a tremendous disadvantage.

Low Debt Levels:

I love when I see a company with no long term debt. Not only does it lend itself to the operational effectiveness of the business (in that they have not needed to borrow money), but the underlying company still has the option to take on loans in the future if required. They may decide to take on debt to acquire a rival, or to survive through an industry downturn. Companies that have already racked up significant long term debt do not have the same flexibility.

What is a good sign: No debt. Another good sign is companies that have been paying their debt down quarter over quarter. Generally this money to pay down their commitments is coming from revenues, but it can also come from other sources like the sale of assets, or subsequent stock offerings.

What is a bad sign: Increasing debt load. As well, if a company has to factor in major payments every quarter just to meet their interest requirements on the debt, it will endlessly hamper the company's earnings until they have negated the loan.

Insider Trading:

This can be tremendously helpful in some situations. However, it is the most over-used and most misunderstood fundamental concept out there. While it is true that company directors often buy shares or sell shares based on their perception of the company's future, they just as often trade for other reasons, and it is impossible to tell which is which.

In addition, since insiders and company directors do not trade weekly or monthly, it is difficult in most cases to pick up an accurate reflection of their intent. Some CEOs will not make a transaction in their company's stock for years at a time.

Often, the amount of an insider sale is so minimal that it should be ignored. If a CFO sells 10,000 shares at $0.50 each, should traders panic and dump their holdings? I doubt it.

You would be amazed at how bad insiders are at predicting the future direction of share prices. They may be very good at developing strategic alliances, or promoting their new anti-cancer drug, but they do not necessarily know much about stock market investing. I have been around long enough to see insiders load up on shares right before a collapse, and sell holdings before a big run-up.

Having stated my position, I will say that monitoring insider trades can be helpful in certain circumstances, if taken into account with several other fundamental criteria described here. On its own, insider trading is the most useless research tool of all.

What is a good sign: Consistent purchases by several insiders and company directors. At very least, they are financially committed to help the shares increase in value, and have a personal financial stake.

What is a bad sign: Share 'fire-sales' with CEOs and directors dumping large lots. Besides the underlying panic about the future of the company, the high selling volume could drive prices lower.

Buy Back Plans:

When a company commits to buying back shares, it is almost always a great thing for shareholders. What generally happens is that a company will use current funds to acquire a certain percentage of its shares on the open market. The shares will be bought over a specified time frame (usually a year) and once bought will be retired (meaning 'eliminated').

While this decreases the company's cash position (which is bad), it reduces the number of outstanding shares (which is good, because the percentage of the company each share owns is greater, thus each share is more valuable). It also provides buying pressure to the market, and states the belief that company directors feel their shares are undervalued at current levels.

In theory, as a shareholder you would want every share besides your own to be retired. Then you would own 100% of the company, certainly an improvement of the underlying value per share.

What is a good sign: Consistent buy back plans year after year, where the company continually gobbles up 5% or 10% of the outstanding shares.

What is a bad sign: Instead of buying shares back and retiring them, they are continually dumping new shares onto the market, by selling new public offerings to raise money. This is also known as share dilution.

Industry Conditions:

The key underlying forces that drive a company's industry will also drive the company. If you invest in a gold mining corporation, swings in the price of gold will be as dramatic upon the penny stock shares as the company's own earnings and revenues.

What is a good sign: A hot sector that is lifting all the involved companies is always fun. What is better is predicting which sector will be hot before it takes off (and being correct).

In 2001, OPEC (Organization of Petroleum Exporting Countries, which include Iran, Iraq, Egypt, etc...), along with support from Russia and Mexico for the first time, stated that their intention was to keep the price of crude oil between $22 and $28 a barrel. They would ensure this through control of the global supply, meaning that production cuts and increases would be used to influence the prices.

(On a side note, OPEC didn't do a very good job keeping oil prices within that range, did they? Recently we were staring at prices of $80/barrel!)

Whenever the price fell very far below this target $22 level, I felt certain that OPEC would follow up at the next meeting with a supply cut. By featuring shares in oil exploration and recovery companies, I was able to help my subscribers get involved early.

Not only were the companies I liked trading at very inexpensive levels because of the low oil price, they were also still making money in the currently difficult market. Sure enough when the OPEC decision came through (you could set your watch to it), the oil sector would be given a boost. This gave the companies I had featured a primary pop in price. The companies would then get a secondary pop as the price of oil began to rise in response to the cuts, and those companies began boasting greater revenues and earnings.

What is a bad sign: Often it does not matter how well an individual company is doing if the entire sector is falling. Even a gold company that is making good money could see itself sinking as traders pull their cash out of the entire sector.

Institutional Holdings:

Other companies, venture capitalists, and even investment institutions can own shares in a company. These 'institutional holdings' represent the percentage of shares of the underlying company that is being held by such organizations.

What is a good sign: Venture capitalists and investment houses feel strongly about the company's prospects and are holding shares for the long term, or are increasing their positions.

What is a bad sign: If a major institutional shareholder decides to liquidate a large position in the stock, it can send the equity into free fall. This may also reveal that they have seen something that they do not like, or are uncertain of the company's future.

Political or Social Shifts:

Businesses arise to fill needs of companies and consumers. As the needs change, so too do the companies filling these needs. A major change in government policy, even a shift in social values, can have dramatic repercussions.

What is a good sign: Increased military spending will help certain defense contractors, as long as they are in the correct arm of the military service business. The sudden commitment to build a multi-billion dollar Star Wars defense system will literally create some companies that previously did not exist.

When the September 11th terrorist attacks happened, social opinion and government policy both shifted significantly. Once the markets reopened, some of the defense and security stocks I had previously featured were instantly caught up in a wave of buying (while at the same time sellers disappeared).

Command Security (CMMD) spiked mainly on speculation, even though they saw little tangible increase in revenues or earnings.

Paravant Computers (PVAT), one of my long-time favorites, also spiked sharply and held onto the gains well, as they were the beneficiaries of increased defense spending.

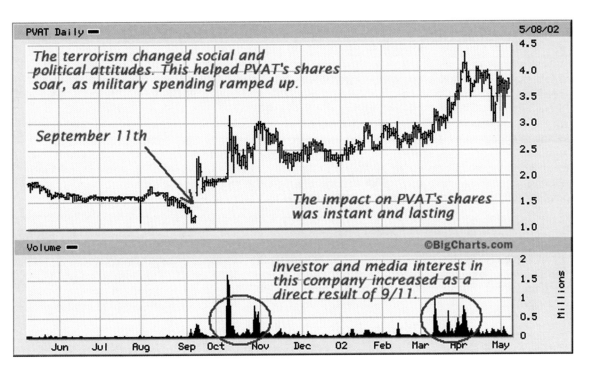

PVAT Daily ▬   5/08/02

The terrorism changed social and political attitudes. This helped PVAT's shares soar, as military spending ramped up.

September 11th

The impact on PVAT's shares was instant and lasting

Volume ▬   ©BigCharts.com

Investor and media interest in this company increased as a direct result of 9/11.

What is a bad sign: Social trends create new business needs while disintegrating others. I do not see many fur coats or horse-drawn carriages around any more.

News and Press Releases:

Read what the company is saying about themselves, and what others are saying about the company, and the industry. However, always consider the source.

Some companies pay web sites to promote their stock, so the editors will say whatever they can think of just to get you to buy shares.

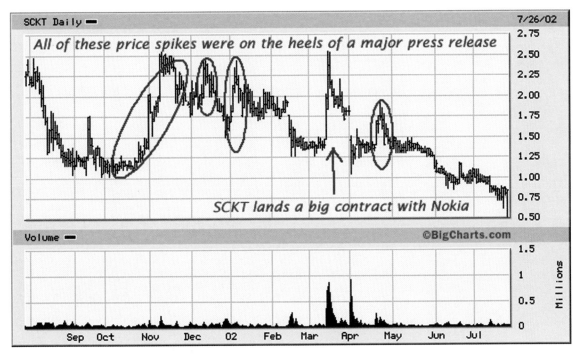

SCKT Daily ▬   7/26/02

All of these price spikes were on the heels of a major press release

SCKT lands a big contract with Nokia

Volume ▬   ©BigCharts.com

Details on the best places to get news releases and press coverage for penny stock companies can be found in Chapter Seven.

What is a good sign: Coverage of the company by major newspapers or relevant trade magazines. Positive earnings releases and quarterly financial reports. Major announcements of FDA approvals, new strategic alliances, share buy-backs.

What is a bad sign: Little or no news is a depressing thing to see, although it is all too common among penny stocks. A company should try to create a buzz with ongoing and exciting advances. Good public relations will help increase awareness of their company, and hopefully generate more buyers for their shares. At the same time, they are showing their accountability by keeping investors and potential investors informed.

By far, the best company for public relations / news releases I have ever seen (and a company which I recommended to my subscribers) was Xybernaut (XYBR). Their interesting technologies allowed for endless public relations hype, and most of their stunts and demonstrations were picked up by major news agencies without XYBR having to do much begging. What the company's wearable computers could do, and the potential applications, was news.

In addition, it was further news when the company's technologies were actually put into use, as they were almost always high-profile clientele. For example, XYBR made hand-held technologies that enabled shorter line-ups at stadiums and airports. It was the stadiums and airports doing the press releases, trying to tell the world how clever they were, and how much better it would be for patrons, while all the time they were selling the benefits of XYBR!

AlarmForce (AF on the TSX), a small burglar alarm-monitoring company, did an interesting thing to help generate investor interest. Each radio or television advertisement that they ran noted at the end that they were a publicly traded company. The ads helped increase sales of their service to consumers and touted the stock to investors at the same time, without any increase in cost. Very smart, while demonstrating a commitment to increasing their share price. This won them a first look from me, and although I had to pass on the stock, I was impressed by the tactic.

New Alliances:

When two companies co-operate, they usually (though not always) find a way to help each other make more money. A great example of this would be Yahoo! and the Associated Press. Yahoo! gets the AP news feed to increase the value of their site for surfers, while not having to pay out for in-house production, or for information from another service. The Associated Press instantly gains an incredible reader base. When I was interviewed by the Associated Press on the Enron situation, it was great to see my news story on Yahoo! the next day.

What is a good sign: If the alliance makes instant and obvious sense (like the one just mentioned above), it is probably a good one. Yahoo! and AP. Peanut butter and chocolate.

What is a bad sign: Too often companies create a new strategic alliance for the sake of being able to use the buzz-words or just to feel like they are making some kind of progress. Be wary of those agreements that do not seem to make sense or do much for the company, especially when they hype it like it will completely change the company's future.

Improving Financial Ratios:

While it is useful to know the price of a stock and the earnings of a company, combining the two into the financial ratio known as Price to Earnings, or P/E, can be even more useful.

You can then compare companies to each other directly, and also get an idea of the earnings power you are gaining for each dollar you put into the stock.

You see, with P/E you can compare 20 different stocks on an even footing. It eliminates the differences in shares outstanding and trading price. You are left with a single number that can be meaningfully compared to the rest.

For example, an analysis of six companies could yield you P/E results of 5.5, 5.8, 6.9, 12.2, 19.8, and 201.0. As lower P/E ratios are better (meaning that you pay less share price for each dollar of earnings power), it would stand to reason that the company with a 5.5 P/E is best from that perspective, while the one with the huge 201.0 result is greatly anomalous to the rest of the companies you screened.

As well, if you see that the P/E ratio (or other financial ratios you use) are improving from one quarter to the next, it should be an encouraging sign.

Personally, I never pick a stock based on financial ratios, but I eliminate them at the drop of a hat if their ratios seem out of whack. If I like a company, strong ratios will reinforce my decision. However, I highly prefer to look at the hard numbers: I like earnings per share (which technically is a financial ratio) more than the P/E ratio, I like looking at total debt more than debt/equity.

Other financial ratios you might want to employ include Debt to Equity, Price to Book Value, or revenues per share, and there are dozens of others.

Note! If you find financial ratios confusing or time-consuming to calculate, do not despair. With highly speculative penny stocks, financial ratios are less important than they are with more conventional equities. They are a piece of the puzzle, rather than a major driving force.

There is a section in the Bonus Chapter which introduces you to financial statements. As well, there are dozens of free websites that will go into much more detail than I will offer here, if you feel you'd like to learn more.

Financial Ratio Cheatsheet		
All of the following ratios can be calculated using numbers available in the company's financial statements. The symbol "-----" below represents "divided by"		
Current Ratio	A company's ability to meet its debts and obligations. A strong company should have a current ratio of 2.0 or higher.	Current Assets ----- Current Liabilities
Quick Ratio	A company's ability to meet its short-term debt, with liquid capital and easily accessible assets. Most companies should have a quick ratio of 1.0 or higher.	Current Assets - Inventories ----- Current Liabilities
Return on Assets	This number tells you how effective a business has been at putting its assets to work. The ROA is a test of capital utilization - how much profit (before interest and income tax) a business earned on the total capital used to make that profit.	Net Income ----- Average Total Assets
Return on Equity	The income a company brought in, compared to the company's 'value' to shareholders.	Net Income ----- Stockholders' Equity
Profit Margin	The gross profit margin ratio indicates how efficiently a business is using its materials and labor in the production process. It shows the percentage of net sales remaining after subtracting cost of goods sold. A high gross profit margin indicates that a business can make a reasonable profit on sales, as long as it keeps overhead costs in control.	Net Income ----- Total Sales

Inventory Turnover	This ratio tells how often a business' inventory turns over during the course of the year. Because inventories are the least liquid form of asset, a high inventory turnover ratio is generally positive.	Cost of Goods Sold ----- Average Inventories
Debt to Equity	This ratio indicates how much the company is leveraged (in debt) by comparing what is owed to what is owned. A high debt to equity ratio could indicate that the company may be over-leveraged, and should look for ways to reduce its debt.	Total Liabilities ----- Total Stockholders' Equity

Besides the select list included above, there are literally dozens more financial ratios. Each has its own place and application. If you are interested in learning more about financial ratios, although their effectiveness is somewhat limited in terms of speculative penny stocks, there are many sources both online and offline.

What is a good sign: Having a lower P/E and Debt/Equity ratio than other companies in the same industry. Improving trends in the financial ratios from one quarter to the next.

What is a bad sign: If one of the financial ratios is far out of whack, it could send the whole company toppling. If you find a debt/equity ratio that is above 2.0, and is far higher than the other penny stocks in the same sector, it may be cause for alarm.

Chapter Three:
Leeds Analysis - Secondary Fundamental Considerations

Market Risk:

It is often difficult, though not impossible, to make money in a downward spiraling market. Of course, it is much easier to bring in the profits when the stock exchanges are roaring along. Just like tides throw the fish around, stocks are inevitably going to be tossed about by the market.

Always remember to compare your success (or lack thereof) to the performance of the markets themselves. Gaining a 5% return in a year that the markets lose 15% is pretty good, even if it does not appear so on your account statement.

Industry Risk:

Every sector of the economy has its own influences. The steel industry is affected significantly by steel prices. Companies based in Texas are affected by laws and regulations that apply in Texas. Defense technology companies are moved by changes in Federal defense budgets.

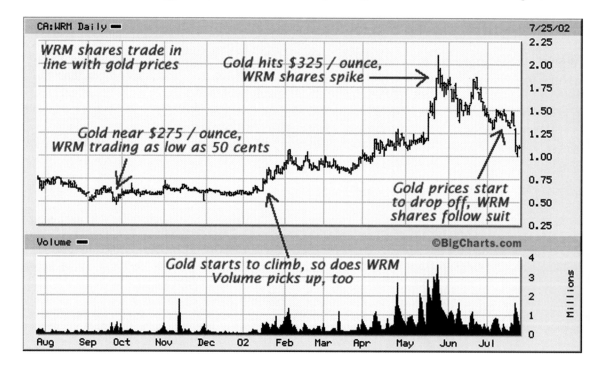

You need to know the potential risks (and benefits) that affect the underlying stock you are interested in. You also need to know the sub-sectors that the companies you like fall into.

For example, a company may be in the diamond exploration sector, and be ruled by all the subsequent market influences, but it may also be listed on the NASDAQ SmallCap market, with a head office in California, and have most of its operations based in South Africa. That company will then feel the influences of changes in NASDAQ SmallCap listing requirements, new rules imposed by California's governing body, and factors that impact the South African diamond exploration business.

Legal Action and Law Suits:

Nothing takes the wind out of the sails of a company, especially a penny stock corporation with a small market capitalization, like being on the wrong end of a law suit. It can cause anything from distraction to destruction, and the uncertainty that goes along with it inevitably causes damage to the share price.

While you can usually find out ahead of time which companies have an existing law suit against them, it is nearly impossible to predict future lawsuits. Even the corporations that get sued do not necessarily know they are going to get sued, so there is no way that an outsider can know ahead of time. For this reason, all I will say on the matter is to factor existing law suits into your company analysis, and do not really worry about unexpected ones beyond that.

Of course, sometimes looming lawsuits can help you get involved in a penny stock for much less than you would otherwise have to pay. When Navarre (NAVR) had a law suit against them thrown out, it helped share prices spike higher. The uncertainty around the litigation had held shares down so long that the response to the dismissal was very strong.

Competition:

New competitors, especially those backed by cash-rich mega-corporations, are often a bad sign for penny stock companies. On the other hand, the failure or disappearance of a competitor will have tremendous benefits in both the short and long-term.

Look for those penny stocks that have claimed and perfected their own niche, and enjoy customer loyalty. There may be a lot of computer manufacturers, but for many years Paravant Computers (PVAT - NASDAQ) solidified its niche by selling rugged laptops and war games hardware to the military. While no other company could outdo them in their own niche, Paravant enjoyed excellent earnings and market growth, even while their major, well-known competitors lost money going head-to-head in the personal computer business.

Management or Board Changes:

Changes in the key personnel can be a good sign or a bad sign. When the company is floundering and needs new direction, bringing on experienced individuals to fill the major roles can often improve the operations of the company.

If the CEO and founder of the corporation, and the only one who really knows how their widget works, suddenly jumps ship, you may want to examine the reasons why, as well as the potential implications.

In either case, such moves do not always impact the share price in the near term. Much of the time investors grade the new management by their results, and give them a chance to prove themselves.

You have now been introduced to the first half of Leeds Analysis. Using the fundamental parameters discussed, you should be able to research any penny stocks you are interested in, and get a pretty good idea of which are the best companies.

Of course, even the best companies are sometimes too expensive. So far, you have found the best penny stock companies. Now, lets get involved in these at the best prices. In the next section, I illustrate some Technical Analysis techniques that you can apply to pick up shares at the low end of their price ranges.

Chapter Three:
Leeds Analysis - Technicals

We have learned how to discover the best penny stock companies in Leeds Analysis (Parts One to Four). Now, let me show you how to get those companies at the best prices.

As I mentioned earlier, technical analysis is the examination of the trading activity in order to (hopefully) predict the direction the stock may take in the future.

Depending on the type of analysis, and the tools used, TA has had varying degrees of success. One of the major problems of using the past to identify the future is that past patterns and trends can change at any time.

Until now, TA could not be applied to penny stocks, because the low trading volumes and small market capitalizations negate the theories.

However, my company has developed our own TA methodology with the specific purpose of applying it to thinly traded penny stocks. We have enjoyed tremendous success with it now for many years. Over that time we have also refined and fine-tuned the strategy.

Look for the following TA patterns and trends in penny stocks that you may be interested in. Details about where to get trading charts for the penny stocks you are interested in can be found in **My Picks for High Quality Web Sites**.

Dip:

Sometimes a penny stock drops sharply by 10% to 30% (or more in some cases), but the dip is based simply on a temporary lack of buying demand. (Or alternately, a sudden increase in the amount of selling volume). Because penny stocks are thinly traded, they are very subject to such 'buying opportunities.'

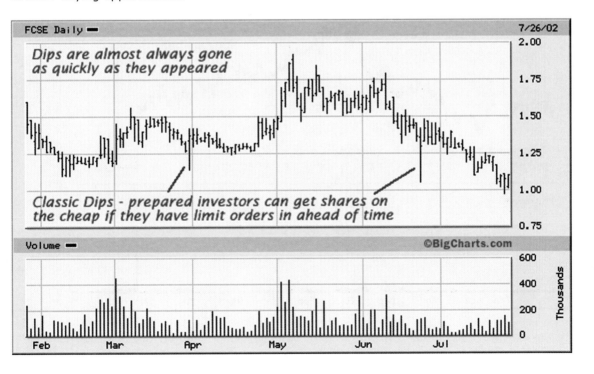

If the dip is not based on a deeper problem, it can be an excellent opportunity to accumulate shares. A true dip is both temporary and unfounded. Investors who get involved in a fundamentally strong penny stock by buying into these dips are generally looking at profits of 10% to 20% within a matter of days.

Generally, the trading volume may be very light at the time of the dip, further solidifying the idea that the price slide was brought on by a lack of activity, as opposed to a panicked sell-off.

Collapse:

The danger here lies in the fact that a collapse looks exactly like a dip. The difference is that the collapse is permanent. Often a collapse is brought on by fundamental factors, such as a law suit or a poor financial release.

In some cases, however, a penny stock has just been 'over reaching' its true value, and once the over-ambitious buyers get all their shares with no regard to the company's true value, and the buying dries up, there is nothing to help maintain the prices.

You should be able to avoid collapses by getting involved with fundamentally strong penny stocks. If the company is already bringing in earnings for an excellent P/E of 5.0, it is less likely that it will collapse and force the already strong valuations down to something absurdly attractive like 3.5.

(Note: I have seen this happen with a stock I owned, called Wheaton River Minerals. The P/E ratio was already very strong, then when the stock dipped it became ridiculous. I had patience, and eventually the shares more than quadrupled).

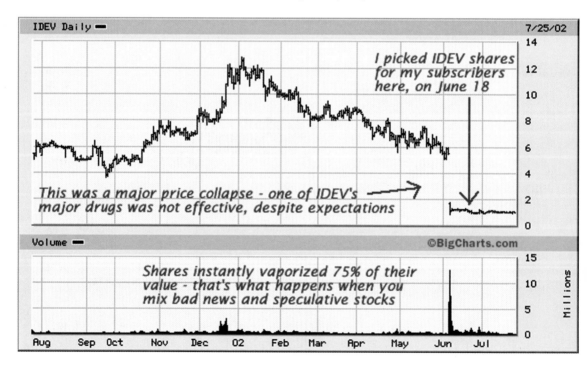

However, if what you thought was a fundamentally excellent company suddenly collapses and does not recover, you may be missing something.

Temporary Spike:

I have seen this all the time, especially with biotech companies, and it is usually fueled by an FDA approval or an appearance at a convention. Sudden buying pressure sends the stock higher.

In almost all cases when the spike is fueled by speculation, it quickly deteriorates. Generally, a penny stock will see a significant gain on the first day of the spike, then lesser gains on each subsequent day, until you see profit taking (people selling at the newly inflated prices) that causes the stock to give up almost all of the previous rise.

If you are looking to make a quick profit on the underlying stock, this is an excellent exit opportunity.

Temporary spikes are often identified by surges in daily trading volume, which deteriorates in line with the momentum of the price rise.

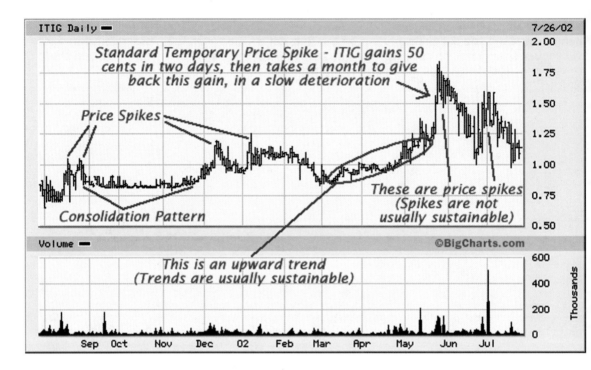

Permanent Spike:

When a fundamental factor drives the spike and it takes place over a longer time frame, (and usually in a less dramatic fashion than the temporary spike), it could be a permanent spike. While there have been many cases where a permanent spike sent a stock 50% or 100% higher in only one day, the reason is usually very obvious (ie- increased earnings announcement, landing a major contract that will be accretive to future earnings, etc...).

When the cause is not so obvious, you will usually see the spike form over the course of a week or so. This may just represent an increase in valuation by investors, and may not be based on anything tangible or obvious.

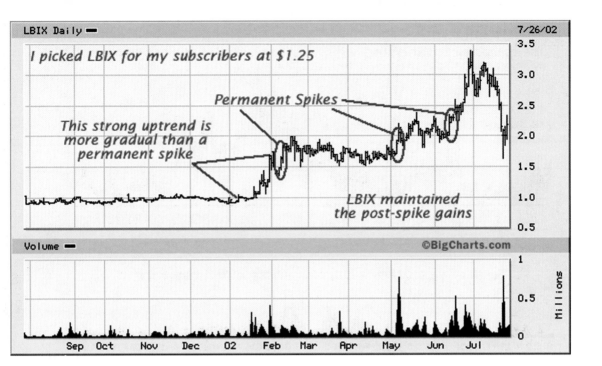

LBIX Daily ▬   7/26/02

I picked LBIX for my subscribers at $1.25

Permanent Spikes

This strong uptrend is
more gradual than a
permanent spike

*LBIX maintained
the post-spike gains*

©BigCharts.com

Volume ▬

Millions

Sep Oct Nov Dec 02 Feb Mar Apr May Jun Jul

Support Levels:

Some penny stocks enjoy support levels, which are prices that the shares do not fall below, due to buying pressure.

Often with penny stocks the support level will form at a marker price, like $1.00 or $1.50 (as opposed to $1.12, or $0.83). This is because many people tell their brokers to 'buy at $1.00,' simply because it is a nice round number.

As well, a support level can be created when a company doing a share buy-back decides that they will acquire their stock at that price. Their buy positions are usually large enough to ensure that their thinly traded stock will not fall below that price.

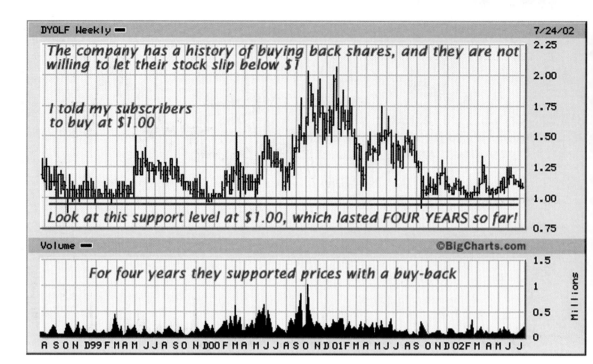

The company has a history of buying back shares, and they are not willing to let their stock slip below $1

I told my subscribers to buy at $1.00

Look at this support level at $1.00, which lasted FOUR YEARS so far!

Volume ━   ©BigCharts.com

For four years they supported prices with a buy-back

A S O N D99 F M A M J J A S O N D00 F M A M J J A S O N D01 F M A M J J A S O N D02 F M A M J J

If this is the case, traders getting in just above the support level (ie- $1.05 in this example of $1.00 support) are facing limited downside risk, while acquiring all the upside potential inherent in the stock.

Often there is a corresponding volume increase whenever shares approach the support. Remember that support levels may increase the chances that a stock remains above the threshold price, but no support level is immune from potentially failing.

Also, it is possible for several support levels to exist for one stock. A penny stock may have moderate support at one price, then even greater support at a lower price, and very strong support at a third.

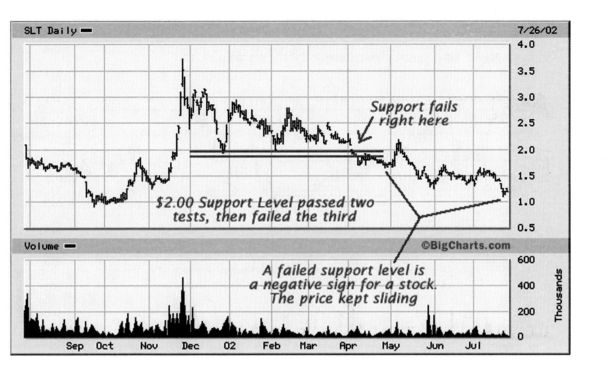

SLT Daily ■   7/26/02

Support fails
right here

$2.00 Support Level passed two
tests, then failed the third

A failed support level is
a negative sign for a stock.
The price kept sliding

©BigCharts.com

Sep   Oct   Nov   Dec   02   Feb   Mar   Apr   May   Jun   Jul

Resistance Levels:

This is precisely the opposite of support levels, and is brought on by an increase in selling activity at a certain price. Resistance levels can be broken through, but they are most effectively used as a way of taking profits from a position for short-term traders.

In many cases, once a trader has identified the support and resistance levels (if any), they can profit again and again by accumulating just above the lower threshold and selling just below the upper threshold. I call this Volatility Play Investing, and detail it in Chapter Four.

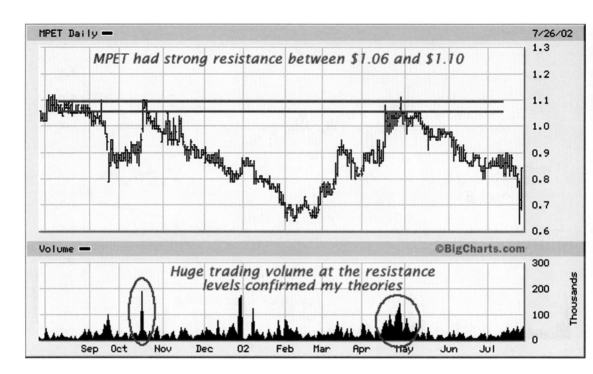

General Range:

By drawing a couple of quick lines on a trading chart, you can usually find the general range that a penny stock trades between. This does not mean that past performance will be continued. However, for some penny stocks it is possible to see that the shares have bounced mainly between an upper and lower price, independent of support and resistance levels.

This range, while it can change at any time, can often serve as a way of knowing what to expect from the underlying penny stock.

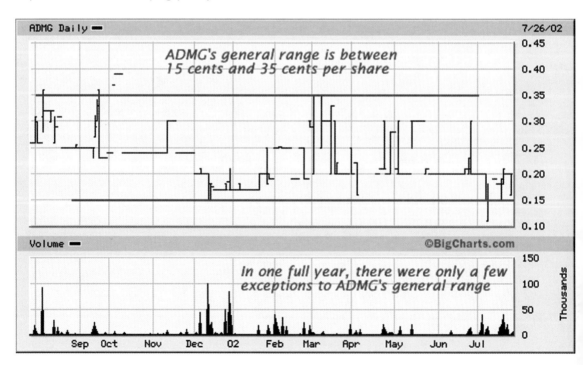

Trend Reversal:

Pinpointing when a trend reverses can be very profitable, and it enables traders (who turn out to be correct about their predictions) to trade penny stocks very near their absolute highest and lowest prices. Having paid less for your shares than anyone else means that you should be in for greater profits than most others.

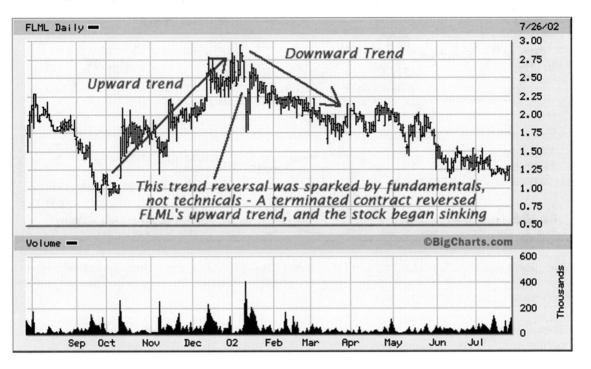

Trend reversals can be a break from an existing trend as mentioned above. However, the most important trend reversal patterns for penny stock traders are topping out patterns and bottoming out patterns.

Topping Out:

After a steep or long-term rise, shares may begin to trade flat across their upper range, giving the look of a flat plateau on a mountain top. Often this can be a topping out pattern, caused by an increase in profit takers selling shares while the buyers begin to dry up. As the daily trading mix goes from mostly buyers to mostly sellers, the penny stock begins to trade sideways, and eventually as the last buyers dry up the stock begins to fall.

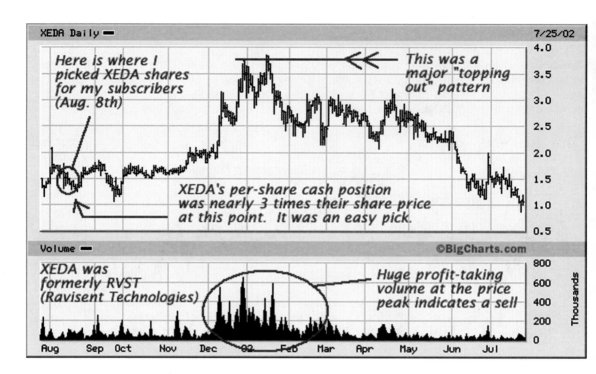

This downward slide wakes up all the other profit takers that had been on the sidelines, who now begin to worry they are missing the boat. The further down the shares go, the greater the momentum that the slide gains.

Often the rise before the topping out pattern, and the fall after, can take as much as six months each. In many cases, a penny stock will top out for about two weeks to a month.

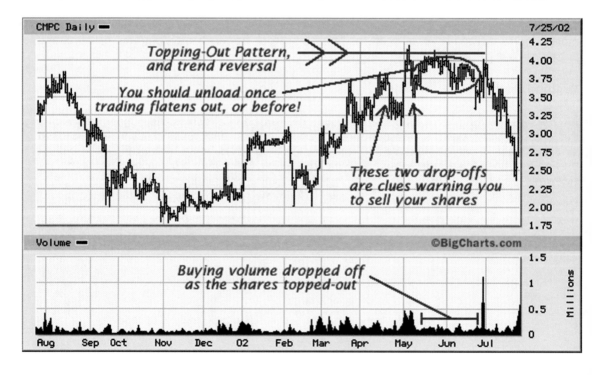

Bottoming Out:

This is almost the exact opposite of the topping out trend, except a stock can bottom for much longer. Former shareholders in the stock sold on the way down, and having been burned by it before are reluctant to get involved again. Buyers after a slide rarely get involved as aggressively as sellers after a rise, and so the bottoming pattern could take even as much as two or three months.

In many cases, you will see that the stock which bottoms out now tops out later. The stock which tops out now, usually bottoms out later.

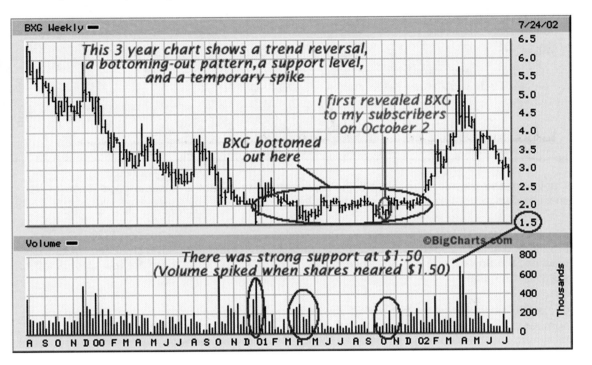

Consolidation:

Consolidations can happen at any point. They often appear after long run-ups, and they can even interrupt the current trend.

When the penny stock trades in a relatively flat range (ie- between $0.40 and $0.55) for weeks, or more usually months, this may be a consolidation pattern. The shareholders that are impatient or disenchanted with their investment are unloading, subduing the effect of the buyers just getting involved.

The longer the consolidation pattern the better. What you want is to see a good turnover in shareholders, with a major portion of the company being held by fresh investors.

You see, if most shareholders have just acquired their stock they are far less likely to turn around and sell. In addition, if most of the long-term shareholders have all exited their position, the upward trend that follows may be unbridled because there are few traders left to sell into the gains.

Check the daily volume for the period you feel may be a consolidation pattern. Add up the number of shares that traded hands the entire time of the pattern, then compare it with the total number of outstanding shares. If 25% to 50%, or even more of the existing shareholders are new, and the stock traded in a narrow range in that time, you may have found a consolidation pattern. If 80% or more of the outstanding shares have changed hands within a brief three or four month window, you can be very confident that it is a consolidation pattern.

Volume Considerations:

In addition to its uses for each of the technical patterns described above, trading volume can also be an excellent technical indicator on its own. Current daily volume compared to previous daily volume levels from months or weeks ago can reveal increases and decreases in trading activity.

With increases in trading activity, unless it is a major sell-off for fundamental reasons, penny stocks usually benefit. They are exposed to higher interest, and the word is getting out about the company. No penny stock quadrupled in price without an accompanying increase in trading activity.

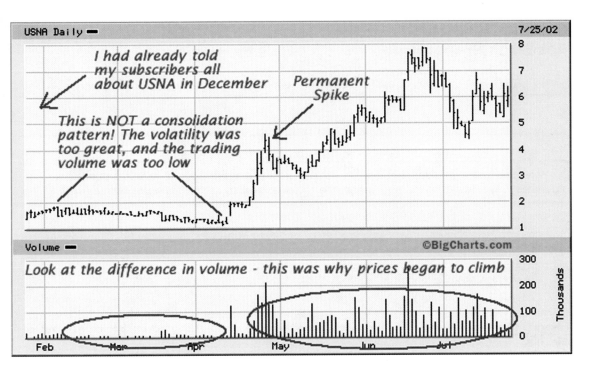

If volume is drying up, especially if it is approaching non-existent levels, you should be concerned. The underlying penny stock may have fallen out of favor with investors, and could see a slow attrition as current shareholders continue to sell into light buying interest.

Chapter Three:
Research Preparation

Before you begin, it is important to know what you expect to get out of your research.

☐   Do you just want one penny stock that will return you 100%?

☐   Are you looking to develop a short list of ten prospective buys to monitor over time? (As a side note, I would definitely encourage the latter approach rather than the former).

☐   Are you just hoping to learn the ropes of finding penny stocks yourself?

☐   Are you going to apply what you have learned to a stock you currently own?

Come up with one single, over-riding goal for your research. This should be the most important reason for doing the work, and the one main thing you want to get out of all this.

Subsequently, list three or four sub-goals that could be benefits from the efforts you are about to expend. Try to keep these goals in mind at all times while doing the research, but don't panic if you also gain other benefits as well!

Applications of Leeds Analysis	
Which of these methods will you be applying?	
Lone Wolf	Apply Leeds Analysis to one single stock. Decide whether or not the company is a good investment based on your research findings. This will help you realize if the stock is likely to increase in price, and why.
The Best of The Best	Choose an industry sub-group, or a short-list of stocks, and rate all of them after applying Leeds Analysis. This will reveal which company is better than the rest, and will help you rank the entire list.
Stock Screening	Apply Leeds Analysis to a pre-screened list of stocks. If you screen by price and market, you will be able to uncover the best stocks from that price range and stock market.
Quick Fix	If you are very interested in a specific stock, you can apply Leeds Analysis to make sure the company has no major warning signs, and to reinforce your investment decision.
Chemistry Approach	Look for those companies that seem to be strong from most Leeds Analysis parameters, with the many strengths outpacing those few criteria that seem to be weak. Every stock will have a few weaker aspects when Leeds Analysis is applied, so your job will be to find those companies which will perform very well, despite a few shortcomings.

Chapter Three:
Short List Approach

Here is one possible research approach to finding explosive penny stocks.

First, you will need a 'short list' of penny stocks. This list can be one you already have, or you can build a listing yourself by using a stock screener, like those discussed in Chapter Seven.

For example, your list may include 10 stocks recommended by my *Penny Stock Insider* stock picking newsletter, or 5 biotech companies, or 25 stocks under $1.50 per share that have a daily volume of 30,000 shares or more. It is really up to you, based on your own interests and investment approach.

Then apply the concepts detailed in Leeds Analysis to all the stocks on your list.

You may do this to rank them from best to worst, or to rule some of them out.

You could also use the methodologies to ascertain what the stocks are worth, good entry and exit prices, and how you expect the stocks to perform in the future.

Let's assume you have a list of eight stocks. Compare them as follows:

• Firstly, list your stocks down one column of a page, then list the parameters detailed below (ie-revenues, cash per share, debt...) in a row across that page. (There is an example of this further down).

• Secondly, rank the stocks in each parameter category, giving them a score from 1 to 8. (1 is best, 8 is worst) If you have six stocks, rank them 1 to 6.

• Thirdly, add up the total scores to create your list in order of best to worst. (Lowest total score is best)

Any stock that has a major 'warning sign' (or several minor ones) should be removed from consideration.

Cull out the stocks with problems. For example, a company may look great except that it has $2.1 billion in long-term debt. Cross it off the list. A company looks amazing, but there is a major lawsuit against them. Cross it off the list.

There are hundreds of penny stocks out there right now that will be trading much higher in the next few months. Do not settle for a dog. If you insist on the best, you will very often get it.

Also note that just because a penny stock outranks the others on your list does not necessarily mean that it is a good investment. It simply means that it is probably the best from the list. (Perhaps all of the penny stocks on your list are bad). Make sure that you not only find out which are the best investments from the list, but that they are good investments compared to the majority of stocks.

It is not required that you consider all or even most of the following parameters in your research, but the more the better.

Fundamental Analysis: ("The Books")

For the following criteria look for a trend from one quarter to the next, going back as far as three years. Also, look at management comments and future expectations to get an estimate of where the company could be going. (Management often make guidance comments in their financial releases).

- Cash per share
- Earnings per share
- Long term debt
- Revenues
- Revenues per share
- Book value
- Competitive advantages
- Share buy-back plans
- News and press releases
- Financial ratios
- Competition analysis
- Market share (current and realistic growth potential)

Technical Analysis: ("The Charts")

Not all penny stocks, in fact quite few, present technical patterns. It is in SOME circumstances that a pattern appears. Do not 'force' yourself to find one if it is not obviously evident. Also, do not incorporate TA into your research if you do not understand it.

You are looking for buying opportunities with the TA patterns I have described to you, as opposed to learning whether or not the stock is a good investment. Rank the shares in order of which you feel is in a good buying opportunity, and make a note of the price or range you think would be best to acquire the shares at.

Try to identify the following TA patterns. If a pattern is not present, or you are unable to identify one, make a Not Applicable note to yourself.

- Dip
- Collapse
- Temporary spike
- Permanent spike
- Support level
- Resistance level
- General range
- Current trend
- Trend reversal
- Topping out
- Bottoming out
- Consolidation
- Volume

Market Analysis: ("The Shares")

The following information can illustrate the stock's liquidity and level of investor interest. You can also use some of these parameters in your technical analysis.

- The market it trades upon (NASDAQ is best, OTC is worst)
- Shares outstanding
- Market capitalization
- Insider ownership
- Institutional ownership
- Insider trading
- Daily trading volume (average)

Thus, a short-list ranking page might look like this. We have listed only three stocks for this example, but generally you may be using 5 to 30.

Short List Fundamental Analysis Rankings Three biotechs under $1.00 per share			
	ABC Corporation	LMN Ltd.	XYZ Inc.
Earnings/Share	2	1	3
Cash/Share	1	1	3
Debt Load	3	2	1
Share Buy-Backs	(No) 3	(Yes) 1	(No) 3
Market Share	1	3	1
Debt/Equity	1	2	3
Total:	**11**	**10**	**12**

Given the above example, LMN Ltd., with the lowest total score, represents what is likely to be the best choice from the group. However, as the rankings are still quite close in results, you would then use additional criteria and continue your research:

Additional Considerations: ("The Situation")

Beyond the above parameters, you need to consider the following.

- Industry conditions for each stock on the list (current and future)
- Sub-sector conditions (current and future)
- Strength of alliances
- Political and social shifts (realized and likely)
- Market risk (this will affect most stocks in a similar way)
- Legal action
- Management competence and changes thereto
- The market it trades upon (NASDAQ is best, OTC is worst)
- Shares outstanding
- Market capitalization
- Insider ownership
- Institutional ownership
- Insider trading
- Daily trading volume (average)

Chapter Three:
Over-Analysis

You need to take the big picture into account when looking for tomorrow's explosive penny stock investments.

It is unlikely that you will find a company that is outstanding in fundamentals all across the board. (If you do, then you have done something wrong in your analysis).

Instead, you are looking for a chemistry of parameters that make the stock ripe for ongoing growth. Perhaps they have some debt, but you can ignore it because they have just started making money for the first time. Perhaps they do not have any earnings, but that is because they are funneling all of their money into research and development for a new ground-breaking drug.

It is more important with fundamental analysis to rule out the bad investments than it is to find the good ones. As has been said by a wise man, "The pen is more effectively used by crossing out than writing down."

It is a lot like buying a house. When you find that penny stock which really gets your attention, you will know it. Until then, you will see a lot of crap.

You need to analyze trends in revenues and earnings, and be able to tell if any decreases are based on factors that may be reversed by the company, or if they tell a darker story. At the same time, discover if earnings are sustainable, and if the current growth rate can be maintained. Did a company get a one-time payment of several million dollars by dishing off some assets, which then obscures their financial picture, or have they been continually expanding into new markets and growing through sales?

The previous discussion on fundamental analysis is what I suggest you use to discover the best penny stocks. To reveal the most opportune buying and selling prices of those stocks, I encourage you to use our proprietary technical analysis techniques.

Now let's get to my favorite part of *Understanding Penny Stocks*, Advanced Strategies.

Chapter Four: Advanced Penny Stock Strategies

Now we are really getting into the good stuff!

Just note that we strongly recommend reading all of the concepts presented in the previous chapter if you haven't already.

Everything revealed in this chapter builds on those methodologies discussed earlier. These concepts do not hold as much relevance without the proper groundwork, which has already been provided.

In other words, make sure to read Chapter Three, **Picking Penny Stocks**, first.

Chapter Four:
Short-Term Trading

Most short-term trading is driven by impatience and greed. However, the impatient and greedy investors never develop winning short-term strategies.

If you want to trade quickly to make a quick buck, forget about it and skip on to the next section. If you want to trade short-term because you believe that there are profitable trading theories that can be applied to stock fluctuations, keep reading.

Pops and Dips:

Sometimes shares can spike or dip just due to a large trade order. This is because penny stocks are generally thinly traded, and any significant volume will push the stock around. Take advantage of this by selling into the rise, not after. You want to be unloading your shares into the buying frenzy, because in this situation it is better to be much too early than a little too late.

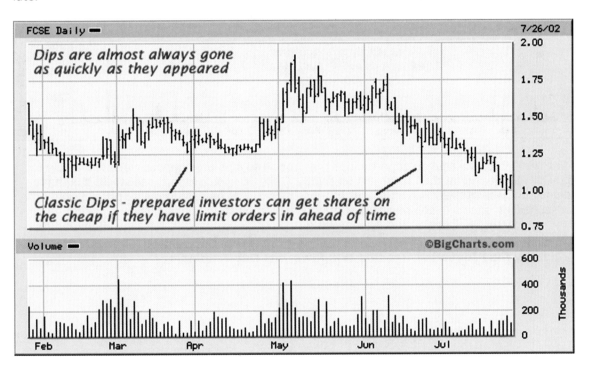

Before you sell, however, be sure to discover if the move is permanent or temporary based on the following criteria:

- **Fundamental Driving Factors:** Tangible impacts like FDA approvals, new mining discoveries, etc, may make the share price jump, and stay higher. Selling into this is not generally a profitable strategy. In other words, if it is a temporary price pop, it may be a profit-taking opportunity. If it is a permanent price increase based on a legitimate driving force, it may be more effective to continue to hold the shares.

- **Subsequent Trading:** You can more readily tell if a pop or dip is temporary, and perhaps a trading opportunity, by closely watching the trading activity. For example, if a price spikes on huge volume, then you notice that the price advance and trading volume are both significantly lower the following day, the spike may be losing steam.

If a dip is on very low volume, it usually is erased as soon as a few bargain hunters jump on the shares. If the dip is on major volume, it may be a sign of things to come. High volume dips usually last, while low volume dips usually do not. Thus, high volume dips are usually a warning sign, while low volume dips are often a buying opportunity.

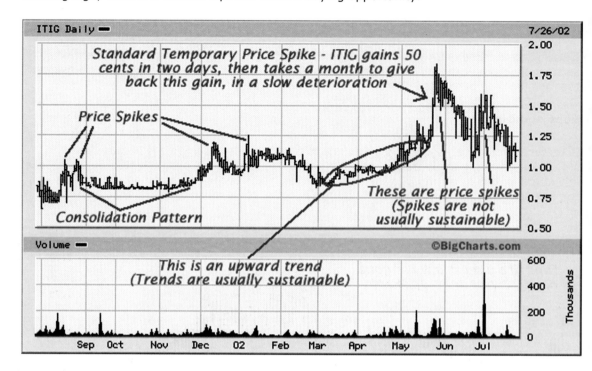

To benefit from the trading opportunities that pops and dips provide, you need to be able to quickly identify them, then react just as swiftly. Take up positions in those stocks that have dipped but will recover. Sell off shares in those stocks that have speculative price-spikes, while holding shares in companies that may be able to sustain their gains.

I provide an examination of short-term trading strategies in this chapter, in the discussions on **Volatility Play Investing, Trading Windows**, and **Day Trading**.

Chapter Four:
Volatility Play Investing

Based on some of the concepts presented in the previous sections on **Technical Analysis**, you may be interested in getting involved with **Volatility Play** investing.

This is a method of trading penny stocks developed by PeterLeeds.com and revealed to subscribers of *Penny Stock Insider*. While other services and traders have attempted to copy and/or resell the concept, no one else has had the success that can be gained by following the concepts that I have perfected.

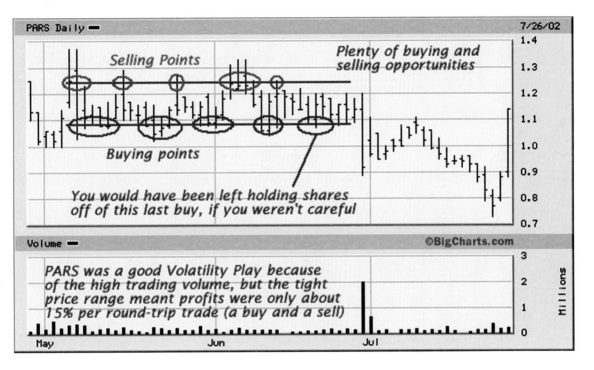

These concepts, detailed below for the first time for public use, allow penny stock traders to make money off of the same stock again and again, by buying near or at the support levels, and selling near or at the resistance levels. (Support and Resistance Levels are both detailed in Chapter Three).

Others have 'butchered' the concept, thinking that any stock can be used as a Volatility Play. They take a penny stock chart and believe that the buy levels should be somewhere near the year low, or perhaps the month low, and that the sell levels coincide with the upper prices the stock has reached.

Such a basic and assuming way of applying these concepts to penny stocks is sure to be disappointing when it comes time to tally your results.

To appropriately identify a penny stock that would be a potential Volatility Play, you need to follow these steps.

1. First, look for a penny stock that has excellent volatility.

A difference from its year high to year low needs to be at least 100%, but some of the best Volatility Plays we have ever uncovered enjoyed a difference of 300% to 500%. This helps ensure a high level of investor speculation and unpredictability in the underlying stock.

2. There also needs to be a pattern of trend reversals.

The penny stock needs to have hit and tested its lower and upper prices several times, preferably two bottom tests and one or two upper tests.

(By testing, we mean that the stock approached its support or resistance level, but was not able to break through and instead reversed. The reversal should take the stock most or all of the way back to the opposite test level. ie - if it tests and bounces off the high, it should then drive directly towards the low over the following trading days.)

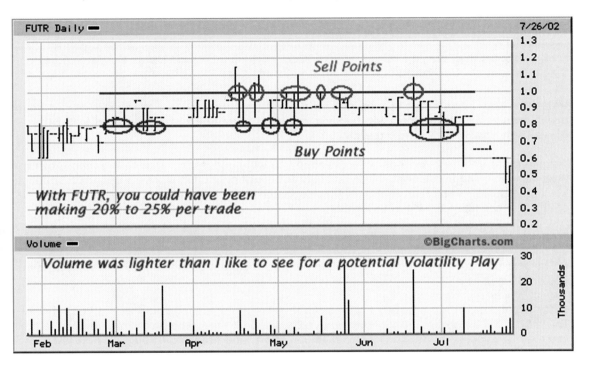

3. The penny stock needs a clearly identifiable support level, and excellent strength at that level.

This does not mean that the support needs to be at a round number, like $1.00. Rather, if a company has just recently announced a stock buy back plan, you can be assured that they will have a lower range at which they intend to pick up shares. If you can identify this level through a surge in volume and a rebound from a certain price, you can expect that there would be good support at that level. While share buy back prices can change over time, most companies will start purchasing at certain prices to keep the shares above a specific level.

In addition, if buyers seem to dip into the market at a certain level, you can usually identify this through increases in volume and a strong rebound off of the support level brought about by sudden buying demand.

A good Volatility Play penny stock always has a strong and easily identifiable support level. This may be $0.45 or it may be $1.00, but you will be able to pick it out easily on the chart through a combination of volume and price analysis.

4. A good Volatility Play penny stock will almost always have an obvious price level where traders tend to cash out and take profits.

Unlike a support level which may or may not be at a threshold number (like $1.00), resistance is almost always at a threshold number for penny stocks.

While a penny stock without a resistance level may just keep rising over time, the difficulty is that you will not know when to take your profits. You will see that a stock without a clear resistance level could reverse on you at any time.

5. A potential Volatility Play also needs good daily trading volume.

Look for stocks that see an average of 50,000 or more shares trade hands per day, rather than averages of 20,000 or 8,000, or 1,000.

Volatility Play penny stocks may not hold their pattern for very many cycles, and can break free at any time. You will benefit more by your ability to pick good Volatility Plays than you will by trading well.

Identify more Volatility Play penny stocks than you will be investing in, with the theory being that you watch the entire flock. Most Volatility Plays will only be in a buying opportunity about 5% of the time. You buy into the ones that approach their support levels while passing on the others that are not reaching your targets.

Timing:

• The best time to buy is right after the penny stock has just bounced off of the support level you delineate.

• The second best time is to buy right before the stock hits support, but has not yet bounced. The shares will be trading only slightly above the support price. The problem, however, is that you may be exposed to the stock price failing support, and breaking through to new lows. If you instead wait for the bounce, it will affirm that the support level has held.

• The best price to acquire shares at is just above the support price. For example, if support is at $1.10, you may want to acquire shares at $1.15 or even $1.12. Don't bother trying to buy in at the exact support price ($1.10 in this example). Don't nickel and dime yourself out of big profits.

• The best time to sell is just before the stock reaches the resistance level. Drops from profit takers can be quick, so it is usually more effective to sell too early than too late. Sell as the price approaches the resistance, not after it has already hit.

• The best price to sell is just below the resistance level. For example, a $2.00 resistance is best sold into at $1.95. (Or even $1.85 to be safe, especially if the penny stock has a history of collapsing back to former levels very quickly).

When investing in this fashion, make sure to factor in the fact that you will be taking more frequent commission charges from your broker.

Also, make sure that the range of volatility is enough to support profits, because you may be buying and selling in a tight price range of only 15% to 40%. If you are making 15% profits on a few hundred dollars, you may only be breaking even after paying trading commissions and taking the occasional loss.

Make sure that the changes in price direction and the degree of price activity are not based on fundamental factors like news releases, changes in financial performance, or other factors mentioned in the discussion on **Fundamental Analysis** detailed in Chapter Three. A company may have been a great Volatility Play, but if it gets a huge FDA approval, the trading ranges can get thrown out the window.

Also remember that you do not necessarily have to sell all of your shares each cycle. This applies even more so if you are not positive about the upper resistance threshold, or you are not even sure if the stock will follow your volatility expectations. You could sell half or a portion of your position, and leave the rest to ride.

As well, you may benefit by gradually increasing the amount you invest in each cycle. If you have made some profits and have a good feel for the stock, and the support and resistance levels have proven out near the prices you expected, you may want to put more cash onto the table.

A Note About Jumping Ship:

If you have pegged a stock's support level at $1.00, and the price breaks through that level, you can know that perhaps:

- Your choice of support level was wrong

- The stock is not a Volatility Play after all, and the concepts presented in this section do not apply

- Some fundamental or technical factor has arisen which has forced a failure of the support level

In any of these cases, it may be best to liquidate your position as quickly as possible, trying to take only a 5% to 15% loss. If you hold every Volatility Play that sinks past your support levels, you will eventually wind up with a portfolio of sinking ships.

The beauty of Volatility Play investing is that you should be taking frequent profits, so the strategy allows for some losses in the interest of the overall picture.

Chapter Four:
Advanced Fundamental Analysis

Beyond the fundamental analysis discussion I have provided you with earlier in *Understanding Penny Stocks*, there are further ratios and methods that you may wish to learn and apply.

I generally feel that these techniques are over-rated, and that they fail to apply to some penny stocks that are driven on speculation, but we will describe them here for you because they may be of value in certain scenarios. It is also a good idea to have a well-rounded knowledge of research techniques as you learn to apply them.

A Quick Secret:

One of the most effective yet under-used research techniques is quite a simple one - contact the investor relations person of the company you are interested in, and ask them some questions you have prepared.

Let them talk and don't interrupt. Often they will lead you to the important information that you need to know, without your having to ask, even if it is off topic from your original question.

Make sure to express your main concerns with the company, and see how they address your tough questions. If they are losing money year over year, ask them how they intend to raise the necessary funds, and when they are going to start bringing in some earnings. If a new competitor has risen up in their sector, ask them for details of their plan to adapt to this new situation.

Listen especially hard for the underlying message that they are providing you with. Are they coming across like a pushy salesperson, or are they confident and excited about the company's prospects?

Go a step further, and contact the investor relations department of the company's competitors. Make sure not to confuse which individual contact-person you liked best with which company has the best prospects. Remove emotion from the equation.

You are the Key:

Do not ignore any specialized or insider knowledge you have in a particular industry. If you are working at an oil refinery, you should know whether your company is expanding or contracting.

If you or a reliable friend/family member is working in the technology sector, you may be able to have advanced warning before they release their next product launch announcement. You may also be able to get an idea of whether or not the new technology has any merit, and if it will be so expensive to bring to market that it breaks the back of the company in the process.

If you are a doctor, perhaps you have the advantage of understanding the technical reports that your favorite biotech company is putting out, and perhaps even whether or not their concept has any appeal or practical use. Do not ignore your own intuition or that voice in your head! If you have a trading advantage, leverage it. If you do not have a trading advantage, admit it to yourself and act accordingly.

Note: None of this is insider trading. You will never get in trouble for it. The misconception that society has about insider trading is far off the mark.

This, among advanced fundamental and technical analysis, is what PeterLeeds.com does professionally. We provide our subscribers with the insights that other traders do not have, and thus enable you to profit significantly. I strongly encourage you to get a subscription to *Penny Stock Insider*, or at least go to PeterLeeds.com and take a look around. I believe you will be both enlightened and pleasantly surprised.

Chapter Four:
Advanced Technical Analysis

I do not agree with advanced TA as it applies to penny stocks.

I have described our proprietary TA techniques in Chapter three, and suggest that you use these, and only these, if you are attempting to analyze a penny stock.

Below is an example of the types of technical analysis techniques that are discussed in *Understanding Penny Stocks*. For a full explanation of all of them, review the section on Leeds Analysis, and specifically Leeds Analysis Technical Indicators.

More advanced TA is unproven even for larger, more heavily traded stocks, and when applied to thinly traded issues like penny stocks, the methodologies are useless and misleading.

Chapter Four:
Trading Windows

Any experienced trader, whether dealing in penny stocks or otherwise, will tell you that the majority of stock gains are produced in short time frames.

In other words, the big 50% and 200% price climbs (and collapses for that matter) often happen in a matter of days or weeks, while the same stock may level out or trade within a narrow range for months at a time, before and after the move.

Most stocks will create 10% or 20% gains over the course of months, then suddenly produce strong 50% or 100% rises in a matter of weeks.

This is especially true when a penny stock is reacting to significant news. Even the most volatile penny stocks may have a trading range that varies 40% to 100% from high to low, but when that news breaks, the price of the shares also break out of the range and soar higher (or lower) within a matter of days... or hours!

To make the most of your money, you may benefit from trying to ride the gains that these windows provide, rather than holding the shares over the longer term and taking the exciting rises along with the drawn-out boredom that can come in between.

There are four ways that we have identified to increase your chances of holding shares just before they make their moves.

1. Technical Analysis Indicators:

As detailed in the section on TA in Leeds Analysis, some trading patterns can help you anticipate a break-out or strong price move to the upside. Penny stocks can often bounce off of support levels, reverse their trends, explode out of consolidation patterns, or bottom out. Each of these technical analysis patterns were designed to apply specifically to penny stocks, and can prophesize the coming of a penny stock price move.

2. Type of Company:

Different penny stocks are prone to different trading activity based on the industry or sector they are involved in, or the type of business they operate.

For example, retail stores have a certain predictability of earnings and revenues that does not allow for sudden explosions of price. Instead, they are more susceptible to longer, less dramatic price trends.

Meanwhile, a biotechnology company can see its share price suddenly double or cut in half based on news (see item # 4 below), rumors, or even rampant speculation. FDA approval? Law-suit from side-effects of their primary drug? The driving forces for a biotech penny stock to see its shares ramp higher are usually dramatic. This is true even if traders do not realize or understand what the FDA approval means for the company, or what the drug actually does!

Other penny stocks that are subject to spiking higher include research and development corporations, companies with inventions that require patent approvals, and those businesses that operate on a contract by contract basis, where one major contract could represent a significant portion of their total revenues. (Defense industry suppliers, for example, often have a few major contracts. They can see their share price thrown around suddenly because of contract awards or losses).

Examples of companies that are not necessarily subject to the same sudden price moves are businesses like restaurants, retail, and entertainment.

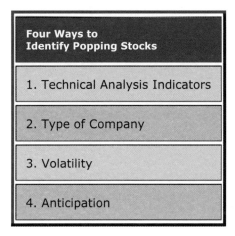

Four Ways to Identify Popping Stocks

1. Technical Analysis Indicators

2. Type of Company

3. Volatility

4. Anticipation

Most other companies fall somewhere in between, and are subject to price moves if the driving forces of their industries suddenly factor in. (For example, a war in the Middle East will affect oil production stocks).

3. Volatility:

Some stocks are naturally more volatile than others, for any of a number of reasons, or sometimes for no conducive reason at all.

To get the most out of these volatile penny stocks, try to accumulate at the bottom of the volatility as detailed in the section on support levels in Leeds Analysis.

4. Anticipation:

It is possible to predict the approximate time when most companies will release their financials (or you could just e-mail their public relations contact and ask). If you expect the details to surprise the street and you get involved before the release, you may be in for a good price ride.

Going one step further, if you can anticipate other types of releases you may be able to benefit even further. For example, many biotech's will delineate their time line for product development, FDA applications, expected approvals, and product sales. Sometimes it is just a matter of reviewing their previous annual report.

By having this information ahead of time you could locate key buying opportunities, just before the company has several upcoming landmark dates. If the price is right, load up on shares several weeks before they are expected to finish the development of their latest product. Certainly a news release can be expected, and in many cases the news release will affect the stock price, even though there are no material changes or surprises that come out of the company.

From another perspective, anticipating the biotech's time line can help you develop exit opportunities if you are hoping to sell shares, and want to sell into some buying strength to get a better price. The same concepts can be applied to stocks from different industries, but the timelines, effect of releases, and results will differ from one sector or type of corporation to the next.

Chapter Four:
Day Trading

This section of *Understanding Penny Stocks* is meant to give you an introduction into the world of day trading.

Day trading is an effective way to make profits on the penny stock markets. Day trading is not difficult to start doing, and by keeping a few key points in mind you may be able to begin turning a profit within a few days of starting.

Before we begin, know this: True day-traders are involved in options and derivatives, which are more volatile and risky than penny stocks and more conventional equities. Thus, it is not possible to "day trade" penny stocks based on the literal definition. However, it is possible to make profits on penny stocks on a day by day basis, especially due to their volatility, and this is what I explain throughout this chapter.

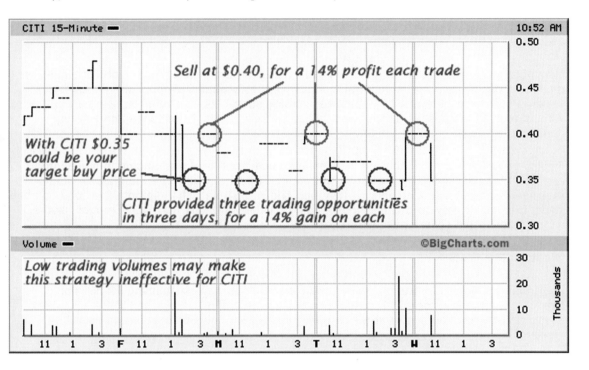

Day trading penny stocks requires a host of stocks (many of these will not make any significant moves from day to day, so it is better to have a whole portfolio of shares to increase your options at any given time).

Each of the stocks on your 'watch list' needs enough trading interest (daily trading volume of at least 50,000 shares), and volatility (Beta factor, as described in the previous section on **Trading Windows**). Note that some penny stocks may have plenty of activity and volatility on a day to day basis, but it can always dry up overnight. Look at average trading volumes over a longer time frame, to make sure that the stocks on your Watch List meet your needs.

Requirements of Investors:

You should not get involved with day trading unless you are able to effectively monitor your holdings and can commit with the proper mind set and outlook. This strategy takes time, research, and a good deal of money (I suggest at least $4,000). Otherwise, you may not be able to benefit from such a trading methodology. If this is the case, you will probably be better off by applying some of the research techniques detailed in Chapter Three of *Understanding Penny Stocks*.

You need to be able to check the prices of stocks on a moment's notice, and get an accurate and up-to-the-minute quote. Having internet access or a computer connection to your broker from work or home is generally best. When day trading, you may need to check stock prices between 6 and 10 times per day. Using a computer it takes only a few minutes each time, you can get current prices, and can alter or submit new orders on-line after checking the stock activity.

It is also important that your stock quotes include the number of bid lots and ask lots when you check a stock price. Most quote services will do this. There will be more about the usefulness of these numbers later.

Most of all, you need patience. Although day trading in penny stocks is probably the quickest profit and loss method in the financial world (with the exception of options/derivatives), patience still comes into play. The best day trading strategies involve often going a week or so without a trade, because you must wait to get the best prices. Impatience immediately negates the effectiveness of the day trading strategy.

Finally, you need a strong stomach. You should understand that day trading in penny stocks can result in one week gains that are monumental, or can set you up for a loss. Whether making a big profit or taking an ugly loss, you should be able to handle both the good and bad stress that will come with this method of trading. Otherwise, you may make moves for the wrong reasons and compromise your objectives.

What Is Day Trading?:

Day trading is simply an attempt to capitalize on short term fluctuations in stocks. For example, with penny stocks it is possible to buy an issue at $0.12 and sell it the next week, day, or even a few hours later at $0.15 giving you a 25% short-term profit on your investment.

If a profit of more than 20% to 25% presents itself, you often take it. Do this a few times and you are looking at a highly successful investment strategy.

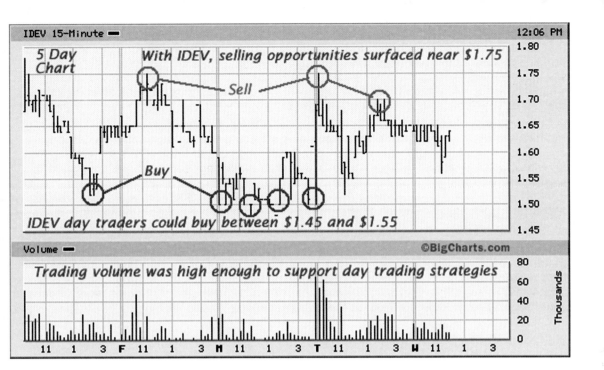

125

The downside of day trading comes into play when you buy an issue and it drops in value. At that point you either take a quick loss to keep your money available, or you sit and wait for a profit opportunity that may arise later, in which case your money is tied up until that time. This becomes less of a concern for traders who have more assets at their disposal, because while only a portion of their money is temporarily tied up in a stock that has fallen in value, the rest of their portfolio could be actively used.

Now, let me tell you how to take advantage of day trading without significant risk, and with maximum profit potential. If you are going to begin day trading, read this next section a few times through and adjust your own investment style accordingly. As well, you may want to start by paper trading.

Goals of Day Trading:

This is very important if you intend to be successful at day trading. Your overall goal is to make several hundred of percent on your investments on a year by year basis. However, this is to be done 40% and 30%, even sometimes 10% at a time. That is where most day trading strategies fall apart - investors don't understand that taking the smaller gains more frequently could actually be more effective than the larger gains less frequently!

Your goals for an effective day trading strategy should be as follows:

• Mainly, to keep on top of your open buy and sell orders, and the trading activity of the underlying stocks so that you are rarely surprised by a stock's action.

• To take small profits when they present themselves. You will find that you have the opportunity for small 15-25% profits very frequently, and you should take these.

You won't often be in a position to be taking the larger 30%-50% profits, because you already would have sold when your shares first began to rise. Therefore, as backwards as it sounds, if you find that you are taking 50% profits more often than 25% gains, you are probably doing something wrong. In the long run, you would likely make more money by grabbing the 25% gains again and again, instead of holding out for the larger returns.

Effective Strategies and Considerations:

The first consideration of this trading method compared to others is that you will taking commissions more frequently. If you are not already with a discount broker, or are paying more than $20 per trade, you probably should switch to a cheaper broker. You can read all about stock brokers, and get my list of the top five brokers for penny stock traders in Chapter Two.

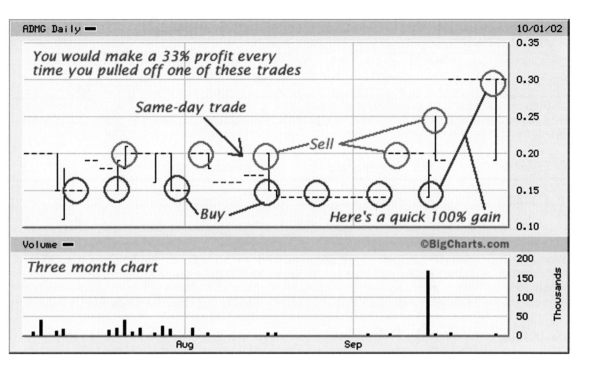

With penny stocks, you may often find that a buy or sell order goes partially filled. For example, you may only get $200 worth of shares and be stuck with a $20 commission. To avoid this, keep track of your orders during the trading day - you may pick up a portion of your order at the price you want, then have to adjust the purchase or sell price to make sure you get the rest of the order filled. Changing an existing order to get all the shares you want on one day, instead of over two or three days, means that you will only be subject to one commission.

The beauty of day trading is that company fundamentals and overall market action become less significant. You are playing the day by day fluctuations instead of hoping the market will rise or the company will increase its earnings. Buying at the low end of volatility and selling at the high end equals success, despite monthly trends, company fundamentals, or the market outlook.

Therefore, it doesn't matter if the companies you invest in have a positive future or are bad long-term purchases. What's important is that you keep an eye on the trading activity of the issue in question, try to pick its higher and lower trading ranges, then execute buy and sell orders accordingly.

With day trading you need to realize that most of your buy orders should go unfilled, because your bid price needs to be lower than the going trading price of the stock. Buy on the dips and you will have success - put in orders to acquire shares at or below the current bid price. If you put in ten buy orders over the course of a month, you may wind up only getting one of the buys you had wanted, but those shares will be yours at a great price, making it easier to unload them for a quick profit.

When tigers hunt, they only catch one meal out of ten attempts.

Deciding on appropriate buy and sell prices at which to submit your orders is relatively simple. Look at a stock that has both high volume of bid lots, and high volume of ask lots. Many people are trying to buy at one price and many people are attempting to sell at another. Look at the spread between the bid and ask prices. If it is about 15% or more, you may want to put in a buy order at the bid price, and if it gets filled immediately put in a sell order at the ask price.

Of great importance is the number of bid lots compared to the number of ask lots. There is a very different stock price outlook if the number of bid shares vastly outnumber the ask shares, or vice-versa. The more bid lots, the greater the buying pressure and price strength at that level. In other words, if there is a large level of demand, the price will likely solidify at that level and begin to climb, unless there are enough shares for sale to meet the demand.

When getting a stock price quote, look at the number of bid lots and ask lots to get an idea of the demand and supply. This will give you a relatively accurate indicator of the direction the stock price will travel in the day, and perhaps throughout the following few days. Use the bid lot and ask lot volumes to help you come up with a price range that the stock will trade within.

Day trading will prove most effective when you trade in stocks that you have been watching for a long time. You will be able to produce better results since you have developed a feel for the upper and lower price ranges. This is not a requirement for success, but rather an advantage.

Hedging and Averaging Down:

As a more advanced strategy, you may want to incorporate hedging into your day trading practices. When buying, this involves putting in buy orders for the same stock at different prices. There is a more detailed look at hedging in the next section.

Let's use an example for the purposes of my explanation. You put in an order to buy 4000 shares of OCN @ $0.23 and a separate order to buy 4000 shares of OCN @ $0.17. Now consult the chart below to see the possible outcomes of your strategy.

Possible Hedging Outcomes
Outcome #1: If the price falls to or below $0.23, your first order gets filled. Now if the price drops further, you may get your second order filled at a lower price, averaging the price of your 8000 shares to $0.20. Profit now by selling at $0.22 or greater. If the price climbs, you will make a profit. If it continues to fall you will take a paper loss. This becomes an actual loss if you sell the shares, or if the shares never return to their $0.22 levels. However, in all likelihood the price will bounce around and will present an opportunity to profit or at least break even at some point in the future.
Outcome #2: The price falls to or below $0.23 and your first order gets filled. The price then rises, leaving your second order unfilled, but providing you with the ability to profit on the 4000 shares you did buy.
Outcome #3: The price does not fall low enough to fill your buy order. You don't get the shares, but you are no worse off. You can extend your order, adjust your prices, or move on to a different stock. An unfilled buy order means that you probably have the right idea. It is better to have an unfilled buy order than to get shares at too high of a price.

These hedging strategies can also apply in the same manner when selling.

Of course, you are also getting exposed to extra commissions with this strategy.

Summary:

Day trading is as straight forward as it sounds. However, you will need a little luck, a lot of patience, and the ability to take the profits that present themselves. By keeping a close eye on the markets and following a simple strategy such as the one outlined above, day trading becomes a straight-forward technical process that requires little thought, yet can provide impressive returns.

Chapter Four:
Hedging

Hedging can involve diversification through accumulation of opposing investments.

So, what the heck does that mean? Well, say you buy into a sector or type of stock that acts in opposition to your current stock holdings, in order to reduce your overall risk. You have just hedged.

Here is another example, which I believe will be even clearer. Let's say you have holdings in a transportation company that can see their profit margins disappear when fuel prices rise. You may then want to buy shares in an oil production company that benefits from higher fuel prices. The two will act in opposite directions to some degree. If the price of oil rises, hurting your transport stock, you will at least have gains in your oil stock to offset these.

Transportation and oil production companies make an excellent hedge complement.

We encourage hedging for traders with larger portfolios (ie - $10,000 and more) when it makes sense to the individual, although it is by no means necessary. Hedging enables penny stock traders to reduce risk while diversifying their exposure.

Examples of Hedging	
In this situation:	**You could hedge by:**
You are concerned about the future of a company in which you hold shares	Buy stock in a direct competitor
Your transport stock shares always do poorly when fuel prices increase	Take up a position in an oil production company
Your biotech shares are a long-shot: They are looking for a cure for AIDS	If they are not successful, buying stock in a pharmaceutical company that has a drug to treat the symptoms of AIDS will help cover the bases. If the biotech company is successful, their stock increase will far outweigh any losses you took on the treatment stock, whose shares would slump once the cure was verified

Hedging is an infinitely more complicated topic as it applies to conventional investments and to option strategies, but for the purposes of *Understanding Penny Stocks* I will only be introducing the concept.

Hedging can take so many different forms and be used for so many different purposes that it could be a book in itself. (Hey, that gives me an idea!)

Chapter Four:
Averaging Down

Averaging down is the process of buying more shares of a stock that you had previously acquired, now that the price has dropped.

For example, you buy 1,000 at $2.00, and the stock drops afterwards to $1.00. If you buy another 2,000 shares at $1.00, your average price per share for the 4,000 units is now $1.50. It lowers your break-even point but increases your exposure.

I have personally seen people average all the way down, with three or four or five new buy orders. They lost their shirts on stocks like Nortel and some of the Internet high-flyers.

As I state in our section on Tips of the Insiders, I do not support the concept of averaging down. In fact, if you abide by the methodology of Limiting Losses that we describe later in Chapter Six, you will not be in a position where you would need to average down.

Bad investors average down, buying more shares of a sinking stock to decrease the average price per share they have paid. This strategy is like throwing good money after bad, and is hardly ever effective. In addition, it magnifies your losses if the stock keeps dropping. Nevertheless, individual investors seem to continually engage in this practice.

Professionals are much more likely to 'Average Up.' They acquire more shares as the stock price climbs and the momentum of the company rises. They see increasing share prices as a confirmation of their research success, rather than a profit-taking opportunity.

Chapter Four:
Short Selling Penny Stocks

Short selling is the strategy of selling the shares first, then having the commitment to buy them back at a later date.

Traders that short a stock are betting that it will decrease in value, so that when they go to fulfill their commitment to repurchase the shares, they can do so at a lower price. Their profits are equal to the difference in price from the original sell to the subsequent buy.

As brokers do not allow traders to short stocks with prices under $5.00 per share, it is impossible to short penny stocks.

This is probably for the best, as I discourage any new or intermediate investors from shorting stocks at any level.

Unlike regular investing, where the most you can lose is 100% of your investment, with short-selling your losses are unlimited.

For example, if you sell short a stock at $6.50 and that stock rises to $85.00, you are legally required to buy back the same number of shares you sold short at that price. 100 shares at $6.50 means you took in $650, but now it will cost you $8,500 to buy them back.

The potential risk of unlimited losses is not appropriate for inexperienced traders.

Chapter Four:
Warrants, Options, Derivatives, and Rights

These are all different types of high risk investments, and we highly discourage traders from getting involved with them. Most inexperienced traders lose a lot of their money trying to learn the ropes, only to find that most experienced traders are also losing money with these.

The true purpose of options and derivatives is for use in advanced hedging strategies.

Warrants and rights are generally given to directors of companies as compensation or incentives.

While you can make money on these types of investments, you should also realize that this is a game for very experienced traders that are applying hedging strategies or have a stake in the underlying company.

You could also make money playing roulette, but in most cases you will lose. I could not suggest with good conscience that you get involved in such trading vehicles.

Having read all of the methodologies and concepts presented within *Understanding Penny Stocks*, you are now an insider into the world of penny stocks. You have the advantage in this field, so why start looking elsewhere?

The penny stock markets will present greater profit opportunities with lower risk than options, derivatives, warrants, and rights. Forget you ever even heard about them.

Chapter Five:
Penny Stock Case Studies

Every penny stock has a story, and you probably won't believe some of them!

Just take a look at all these fun and entertaining penny stocks; many have really impacted society, others have created and eradicated billions of dollars, others have been splashed all over the news during their scandalous journeys.

From the mysterious "suicide" of a Bre-X insider, to the pathetic death of an Energy giant, to the instantaneous evaporation of billions of dollars, each of these penny stocks has a story to tell.

In this chapter on **Case Studies**, I try to impart some experiences onto you. While it may be highly entertaining to read some of the crazy or unbelievable situations that penny stocks have created over the years, remember that there is a moral to every story. If you learn something from each **Case Study**, it may save you from learning that same lesson the hard way.

Let's start off slow and begin with one you've heard of already, **The Rise and Fall of Enron**, and review some of the comments that I provided to the Associated Press about the whole situation.

Chapter Five:
The Rise and Fall of Enron

Enron, once a high-flying blue-chip trading around $90 a share, and listed by Fortune 500 as the seventh largest company in the United States, fell to levels of closer to $0.20 in only a matter of months. Billions of dollars in stock market value disappeared in only a fraction of the time it took to make them.

At the company's height, Enron had 21,000 employees and was the largest natural gas merchant in the country.

As Enron 'became' a penny stock, I personally received numerous questions and e-mails from members of my service about the viability of the stock as an investment. Traders thought they were getting a deal by gobbling up shares of a company for pennies, when those same shares were worth nearly $100 only a year earlier.

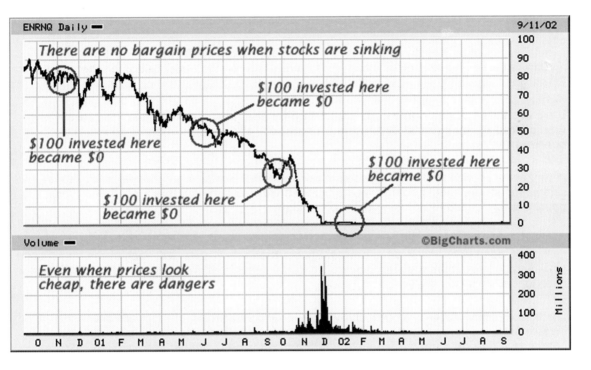

Whether you bought in at 25 cents or $90, those shares are now worthless.

This reinforces a lesson that many bargain hunters choose to ignore again and again: It may have already lost 99% of its value, but it CAN go lower, and it very often does.

Too frequently traders say to themselves, "Really, how much lower could the stock possibly go?" Using that as the extent of their research, they invest feeling secure, and just as if they had bought at $50 or $20, they lose 100% of the money they put in.

**Enron's former Chairman, Kenneth Lay,
testifies after Enron's collapse.**

I was pleased when Kristen Hays from the Associated Press contacted me for my comments on Enron. I was able to use the interview as a forum to provide my position on the entire Enron situation.

Here are some of the comments published by the Associated Press. This interview was picked up by several dozen media sources, and was published on several continents:

Peter Leeds, president of PeterLeeds.com and author of *Stocks That Will Make You Money*, said penny stocks should be discovered before anyone else recognizes a good deal - not bought on the cheap after falling from lofty heights.

Enron descended into bankruptcy in December amid allegations of accounting abuses that included hidden debt and inflated profits. Shares that approached $90 each in the fall of 2000 plummeted to less than a dollar, leaving workers and retirees with depleted 401(k)s that had been loaded with Enron stock.

Leeds said penny stocks are particularly volatile, and 95 percent of them are poor investments. His company tries to find the 5 percent with realistic upside potential, using criteria that include a proven management team, growing revenues and earnings, a low or nonexistent debt load, patented technologies or innovations, and market dominance.

"I would say that Enron falls well short in all of these categories," Leeds said. "From our perspective this rules out the stock many times over."

He said Enron meets the criteria for high trading volume and brand recognition. But the volume decrease since January makes it more difficult to profit from speculative trading. And the name "has a negative connotation and so is an additional strike against the stock," Leeds said.

Even Enron officials have said they will leave the name behind as it reorganizes to focus on its natural gas pipelines and power operations and tries to emerge from bankruptcy.

So, what happened with Enron anyway? To make a long story short, they cooked their books. Vastly understating billions in debt and liabilities, while using accounting obscurities to polish the look of their financials, they set themselves up for a tremendous collapse.

136

There are Two Morals to this Case Study:

• The first is that stocks CAN go lower, regardless of how much they have already dropped.

• The second is that even the professional analysts and money-managers that followed the stock closely can be fooled by crafty bookkeeping.

Chapter Five:
The Bre-X Debacle

When I was interviewed by KPHN live radio about penny stocks, the host of the *Total Business Show*, Scott Simon, asked me to share some of my favorite penny stock success stories. I gladly brought up Bre-X.

While the majority of people have a negative connotation about the stock (the reasons for which are detailed below), I explained that it was actually an excellent investment from the perspective of penny stock investors.

You see, it was the penny stock traders that made excessive profits (and I do mean excessive - thousands of dollars turned into millions) from the stock, while the more conservative and 'safe' investors were the ones who got so badly burned by getting involved late, at high prices.

A Quick History of the Situation:

Bre-X Minerals falsified their core samples from their gold-mining claim in Busang, Indonesia. Simply, they incorporated a process known as "salting" the samples. When a core sample is prepared for examination, it is generally rinsed off. The Bre-X jokers were bold enough to put flecks of alluvial gold (which is harvested from river beds instead of from the ground) into the water they rinsed the samples with. On first glance, an untrained examiner would think that the ground where the sample came from was loaded with gold.

Bre-X once traded as low as $0.04 (in 1991), and on a split-adjusted basis eventually hit levels of $286.50! (Figures are in Canadian dollars, as Bre-X was a Canadian company and traded in Canada before also being interlisted in the U.S.)

While some quick math reveals that $1,000 could have become $7,162,500, it is mainly the dishonest insiders that would have seen these kinds of gains. For the most part, the majority of investors (individuals, institutions, mutual funds...) bought in at prices closer to the top end of the stock's ascent.

While no one has yet been found responsible for the scam, many fingers pointed at Michael de Guzman, the chief geologist who had access to the core samples. de Guzman "committed suicide" shortly after the hoax was revealed, by "jumping" out of a helicopter over the Indonesian jungle. This sentence should probably read, "de Guzman was pushed..." but we'll leave it at that.

The point is that most people who hear about Bre-X instantly react by bad-mouthing penny stocks. However, they got burned by buying it when it was a large-cap, for hundreds of dollars per share. Meanwhile, the penny stock traders who got in at levels below $2.00 made a fortune.

I think that the whole Bre-X fiasco should be a shining reminder of the power of penny stocks. The profit potential is unlimited.

And remember, you and I are not in the business of verifying the accuracy of core samples. We are in the business of making money from our penny stock trades. The truth of the details is far less important than the perception of the details, especially since penny stocks are driven by speculation.

The comments above are not to say that I knew it was all a scam. None of us did. That is the whole point. Getting in early with a penny stock, based upon any reason or rumor, regardless of accuracy, can be a profitable experience.

Even the Big-Name Companies Were Fooled	
Lehman Brothers:	Described the Busang claim as the "gold discovery of the century" and recommended Bre-X as a strong buy.
Fidelity Investments:	The world's biggest mutual-fund company held 7.3% of Bre-X just before the collapse.
J. P. Morgan:	The key investment banker to Bre-X, it was shopping Busang to world mining giants.
Kilborn Engineering Pacific:	The respected Canadian mining engineering firm reported that Bre-X's Busang deposit contained 71 million ounces of gold.
Gold Mining Giants:	Eager to get in on the Busang claim, gold companies tried to woo Bre-X. Placer Dome offered $4.7 billion in a takeover bid; Barrick made its own undisclosed offer. Indonesia rejected both bids in favor of Freeport-McMoRan, which offered to pay $400 million to help mine Busang.
Indonesian Government:	The Suharto regime grabbed 40% of the Busang deposit for the Suharto family and other Indonesian interests. It did not pay Bre-X compensation.

Another Bre-X style scam is much less likely now, especially because of the lessons learned. However, I do not doubt that there will be other scams that are just as brazen, only the theater or delivery method will be something new.

A good penny stock investor knows that it is not important if Bre-X really has any gold in the ground or not. Instead, the majority of investors need to think that Bre-X has real mineable reserves, so that the good penny stock investor can exit his/her position while everyone else gets on board. Profits are made by the reaction of investors to company news, and by the implications of the news.

Chapter Six:
Secrets of the Insiders

What you are about to read has previously been sold for hundreds of dollars per copy.

The concepts themselves are worth thousands. I personally have used these methodologies to reap huge profits from penny stocks, and they are easy to learn!

The following reports may surprise you. But from this day forward you won't be at a disadvantage to all of the insiders and professionals that have been making money off of your bad trades.

Our first section of this chapter is called Extreme Research, and it is not for the feint of heart.

Chapter Six:
Extreme Research

Warning! This is most definitely not for everyone, nor is it necessary in order to benefit from all the concepts and methodologies presented in *Understanding Penny Stocks*.

There are always those investors who are willing to go beyond the call of duty, to make the greatest profits. I call the concept Extreme Research, and it can help you have more powerful and insightful knowledge than 99% of the traders out there.

It also requires getting involved in these stocks and companies to a degree you never expected that you would.

If you knew that the CEO of a company was an alcoholic and that the back wall of his factory was collapsing in on itself, how much would that information be worth to you?

Better yet, when you called the Workplace Safety Board, and knew that would cause the factory to be shut down, you are getting involved to a degree beyond which most investors could even consider going.

In this example, you are not breaking the law, nor are you doing anything more than extreme due diligence. The fact that you may have saved some of the employees' lives is just the gravy.

So how do you make money in this example? Well, you are not investing in the company that is about to be shut down. You are investing in its competitor.

The phone call to the workplace safety board represents the crossing of the line between participant and influencer. Your actions may affect the price of the stock, so you have some influence.

We do not suggest that you become involved in Extreme Research for every single investment that you may make, and in many cases it is not possible, or would have no effect. However, if you happen to know that a company you want to invest in has a head office within 30 minutes of your aunt's place, go check it out next time you visit her. Call ahead and see if you can meet with the investor relations contact there, or even just pick up some of the company's financial statements.

You would be amazed at how often you will no longer invest in a stock you had been gung-ho about, just because you see the office.

(A great example of this can be seen in the movie, *Boiler Room*, when the main character and stock promoter goes to the Med-Patent office. Nothing there but an old sign and an empty building unit).

Extreme Research Examples
You know the security guard from a penny stock company, and he saw several executives from Microsoft stop by after hours. Could be a huge deal in the works, or a takeover target. Either way, there could be a nice pop in the stock. (Especially once you let word get out!)
You know the company you work for is heading south fast, more because of poor management and bone-head decisions than due to sales. Stock in a competitor's company may serve you well, once your employer finishes its 'death dance.'
Visit the head office of a company you are interested in. Do they run things efficiently? Do the employees have good morale?
Buy the product or service of three competing companies, and compare. Is the best one also the least expensive and most easily accessible?

If you happen to know someone who works at a penny stock company, take an interest in what they are saying. In most cases it is best to avoid letting on that you are interested in buying the penny stock, but instead act interested in what they do for work. Find out how employee morale is, what does their company lack, who are their competitors, who is sleeping with the boss...

Most of this, or perhaps all of it will be useless. However, when you get that one piece of information that could turn the trading tables in your favor you will know it.

What if your contact complains about managers from a competitor coming around the office, and she does not think they should have any place there because of trade secrets. You would read between the lines, and be able to predict that either the competitor is having managers jumping ship and looking to relocate, or perhaps the two companies may merge or there may be a buy-out, which explains why company A is allowing company B's managers to snoop around. Whether it eventually happens or not, even the breaking of such a rumor can send the shares skyward.

There is no format or methodology to Extreme Research. It depends upon your situation and level of ambition. I will say one thing, though. It works. Just don't do anything against laws or ethics. Extreme Research can be done without putting yourself or your morals at risk.

Chapter Six:
Tips of the Insiders

Professional traders continually make more money than average investors, even when they are trading the exact same stock!

There are specific reasons why this occurs, although it is not hard for the less experienced investor to start making the same kinds of gains that the insiders are getting.

Here are a few tips to put you on an even footing with the professionals... and leave all the average investors behind!

- **Enter your trade orders between 2:00 pm EST to 3:45 pm EST:** Many institutional traders watch the activity of a stock throughout the day, and take market direction, fresh news, and economic indicators into account. Then, after staying on the sidelines and watching patiently, they start moving in. This can cause shares to begin to move under the trading pressure that the professionals bring to bear.

Often, the true direction of a stock's price is influenced more by the trading in the early afternoon than all of the rest of the day's activity put together.

Tips of the Insiders
• Trade between 2 pm to 3:45 pm EST
• Set Maximum Losses
• Don't Average Down. Average Up
• Never Leave Trades Open Overnight
• Never Use Market Orders
• Investor Sentiment is the Law

As well, holding off for the several hours of trading also allows you to benefit from whatever news and press releases hit the market that day. It enables you, like the insiders, to see how investors react to a specific piece of news, then react to the reaction.

In other words, the specific details of a press release, news report, or occurrence is less important than how the market responds to the information. Wait to see what the reaction will be, and then get involved only if it will benefit you.

- **Set Your Maximum Losses:**

Many professional traders set maximum loss limits. Often they sell their entire position in a company if the shares fall (for example) 10% below the price at which they had bought. This eliminates any killer 40% or 80% losses, while keeping capital free for subsequent investment in the shares at a later date, or for other stocks altogether.

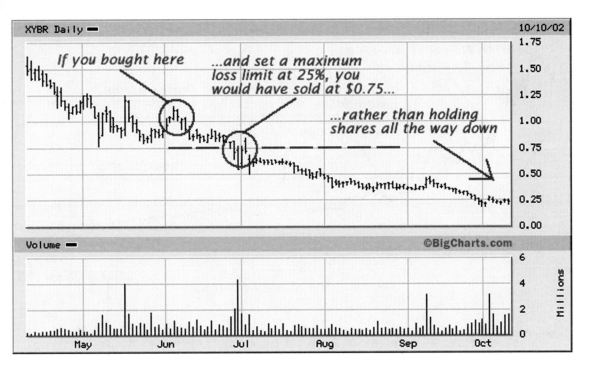

Think of your own personal investment experience. Have you had any losses of greater than 15%? Did the shares rebound or continue to fall. How would your portfolio have performed if your greatest losses had been reduced to 10%?

Unfortunately, keeping to this loss limit is one of the most difficult things for traders to do. There is always the hope that the shares will rebound, and sometimes they do. However, the key is being willing to miss out on those stocks that do rebound in exchange for never suffering a major capital loss again. The insiders take this trade-off 9 times out of 10.

Our next section in *Understanding Penny Stocks* is an entire examination of just this one concept, Limiting Losses.

- **Don't Average Down. Average Up:**

Bad investors average down, buying more shares of a sinking stock to decrease the average price per share they have paid. This strategy is like throwing good money after bad, and is hardly ever effective. Nevertheless, individual investors seem to continually engage in this practice.

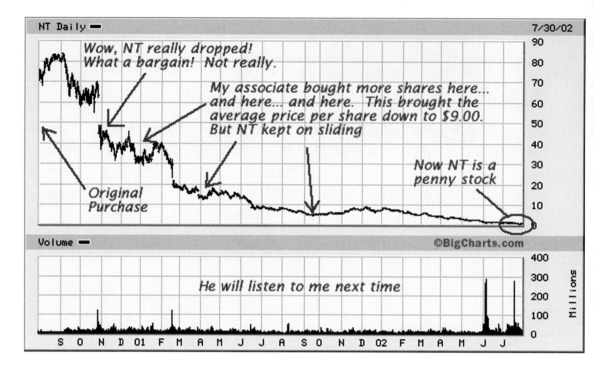

Professionals are much more likely to 'Average Up.' They acquire more shares as the stock price climbs and the momentum of the company rises. They see increasing share prices as a confirmation of their research success, rather than a profit-taking opportunity.

In *Understanding Penny Stocks* we have a complete section devoted just to the theory of Averaging Down.

- **Never Leave Trades Open Overnight:**

Professional investors seldom leave buy or sell orders open past the end of the day. Any number of things can happen which will (or should) influence you to change the price you have put forward. It is never good to commit yourself.

For example, if you are selling and there is a sudden press release which sends the share price soaring, you get bought out at your target price, and miss out while the stock continues to rise. However, if you did not have your open order you could have sat back until the smoke cleared, and then made your sale at a higher price.

In addition, there is often a build-up of buy or sell orders overnight. This is because many investors can only enter their trades after work, and there is no fulfillment while the markets are closed.

This can cause a major problem when the exchanges do open, as a clump of simultaneous buy orders can often lead to a 15 minute pop in share price during this temporary demand. If your order is one of these, you may wind up paying more than you had intended.

Generally, after the order fulfillment has recovered, the share prices settle back down to their previous level. This also applies in reverse when a lot of sell orders have been accumulated.

To avoid this situation, use limit orders (see below) and use orders that expire at the end of the day, instead of ones that are open over several days at a time.

- **Never Use Market Orders:**

We have a complete examination of market orders and limit orders in Chapter Two of *Understanding Penny Stocks* in the section on Trading Stocks.

The use of limit orders (setting a specific price at which you are willing to trade shares) enables you to protect yourself from the volatility of the stock market.

Especially when dealing with lightly traded stocks, a market order (trading shares at the current best price available) can result in paying more than you would have agreed upon. Setting a limit ensures the price point, and therefore protects your capital.

Although market orders usually incur smaller broker commissions, the savings generally fall short of the capital losses brought on by their use.

There are Two Types of Orders You Can Use to Trade Stocks:

Market Order:

You want to trade shares of a stock, and are willing to pay whatever the best available price is. You will be assured that you will get the stock, but you have no guarantee of the price you pay.

Limit Order:

You want to trade shares, but are only willing to make that trade at a certain price per share. For limit orders you need to set a price limit.

Market Orders	Limit Orders
You will take the best available price	You will only buy at the price you stipulate, or one that is even better for you
You do not need to specify a price or a time when the order will expire	You must specify the price you are willing to pay, and the date at which your order expires if it is not first filled
You instantly get your shares	You may have to wait, or the trade may not even happen at all, if there are not sufficient shares being sold at the price you stipulated
You will get all the shares you wanted	You may get a "partial fill" (meaning that you only get some of the shares you wanted) if there were not enough shares for sale at the price you picked
You may end up paying more per share than you had wanted, especially if your buy order is large, or the underlying stock is subject to low trading volume	You control the price, and protect yourself from unexpected volatility
I highly discourage the use of market orders, especially with penny stocks	I always recommend using limit orders with penny stocks

- **Investor Sentiment is the Law:**

Stock prices have more to do with investor sentiment than corporate operations. Most investors read a press release and ask, "how will it affect the company's bottom line?" It is more effective to ask, "how will this news affect the way investors see the stock?" or "how strong will the reaction of traders be to this news?"

Trying to make money off of a company's operations is never as effective as making money off of other traders. An increase in earnings does not DIRECTLY impact the value of your portfolio. An increase in the share price due to traders buying up the stock does.

Make money off of the moves of traders, using the underlying companies as a vehicle to enable your strategy.

Chapter Six:
Limiting Losses

It is said that the pen is more effectively used for crossing out than for writing down. Similarly, success in stock market investing is often generated by effectively minimizing losses rather than by riding the gains.

All investors will encounter losing stocks. However, the amount to which these damage a portfolio depends on how the investor handles them. The proper placement of stop loss orders and effective diversification can significantly bolster one's portfolio against the downward pressures that often affect individual stocks.

Preservation of capital is the key. If the most you could lose on a single trade was 2% of your overall portfolio, it would take many, many bad trades before you lost your shirt. And this is assuming that you made no beneficial trades in that time frame.

As theoretical as this sounds, it is relatively simple to implement such a strategy, such that you limit your losses to minimal levels. However, there are surprisingly few investors who do take on such a strategy.

Attitudes that falling stocks "can't go any lower" or "will have to turn around eventually" are killers.

As well, thinking "I won't sell until I'm at a profit" could tie up your money when it could be making profits elsewhere. Why hold on to a falling stock, when you could have cut your losses earlier, then bought it at a bargain once the slide had ended?

On the stock market it is impossible to always avoid stocks that go down after you have bought them. It is not impossible, however, to limit the losses from these to insignificant levels.

The two underlying principles to implement this strategy are price barriers and stop loss orders. If you are a new investor and these terms seem daunting, rest assured that the concepts behind them are very simple.

Note! For many penny stocks, especially OTC-BB issues, your broker will not allow for stop-loss orders. This is yet another reason to stick to penny stocks that trade on the NASDAQ and AMEX, since you may be able to use stop-loss orders.

Note Number Two! I generally do not suggest the use of stop-loss orders, unless you are an experienced trader and the underlying penny stock has high trading volume and low volatility.

A price barrier is simply a level which a share's price should have a hard time falling through, such as a support level, or lower trend line.

For example, ABC shares may sink to the $1.00 level many times, but may always bounce back up, without ever breaking through to levels of less than a dollar. This could mean that there may be a support level at $1.00. However, there is more to identifying support levels, and charts should be used as described earlier in Chapter Three.

I discuss support levels in detail in Leeds Analysis.

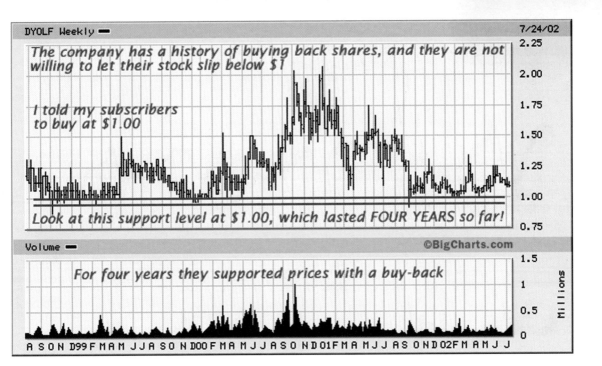

The company has a history of buying back shares, and they are not willing to let their stock slip below $1

I told my subscribers to buy at $1.00

Look at this support level at $1.00, which lasted FOUR YEARS so far!

Volume ━   ©BigCharts.com

For four years they supported prices with a buy-back

The reason support levels exist is because there are stronger buying pressures at those prices than selling pressures, which keeps the share price at or above the support.

The opposite holds true for resistance levels, where the price of a stock may have trouble breaking above a certain point, despite repeated attempts.

The second concept is that of stop loss orders. This is simply an order to sell your shares if the trading price falls below your stop price. If the shares increase in value you will continue to hold them, but if they fall to or below the level where you set your stop, your sell order kicks in and your shares get bought from you at or near that price.

Stops can be used to limit losses or to protect profits. Effective use of stop loss orders has seen some portfolios post a trading profit, despite winning on only 30% of trades. This is because the losses from the 70% of losing trades were very limited, while the gains were allowed to ride, and out paced the minimal losses.

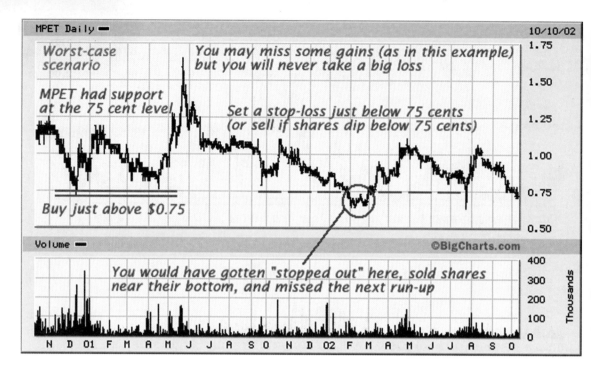

MPET Daily ▬   10/10/02

Worst-case scenario

You may miss some gains (as in this example) but you will never take a big loss

MPET had support at the 75 cent level

Set a stop-loss just below 75 cents (or sell if shares dip below 75 cents)

Buy just above $0.75

Volume ▬   ©BigCharts.com

You would have gotten "stopped out" here, sold shares near their bottom, and missed the next run-up

Stop loss orders can help investors protect their capital in the event of a share decline. Price barriers can help investors identify levels where a share's price may bottom out, or at least will only fall through in the presence of heavy selling pressure.

While both 'unrelated' concepts can act as useful investment tools, it is the value-added combination of the two which generates the tremendous effectiveness of the overall methodology.

Three Steps to Limiting Losses
1. First, identify a price barrier for any particular stock. This can be done through your own research, or learned from professional investment research. For this example, we will assume that stock ABC is trading at $1.15 and there is a long-term support level at $1.00, which ABC has often approached, but has never fallen through. ABC share prices have been falling in recent weeks, therefore approaching the support level.
2. Next, put in your order to buy shares, near to the support level, but slightly above. We will assume a buy of 2000 shares of ABC at $1.03. An even more effective strategy for investors with the time and resources to closely monitor the stock would be to wait until ABC has hit $1.00, then began moving higher, confirming that the support level has held. After this confirmation, put in an order to buy shares as they rise away from the $1.00 level.
3. Immediately after acquiring your shares, put in a stop loss order below the support level. In our example, we would put a stop loss for 2000 shares of ABC at $0.98. If share prices fall to or below $0.98 then your stop loss order will kick in, selling the shares at a loss of about 4% and commissions.

If the support level holds and the price remains above $1.00, you have successfully bought in very near the short term bottom in price. You will be in a profit position as the share's price travels higher, with the added insurance of the support level just below your position.

As the price does rise, you should adjust your stop loss order upwards. For example, if the price passes $1.20 you may want to move your stop up to $1.09, and if the shares rise above $1.40 you may want to increase you stop to $1.29. This concept will help you lock in your profits. You will be able to take advantage of the price climb, and your shares will only get sold the first time ABC's stock price reverses and starts heading south once again.

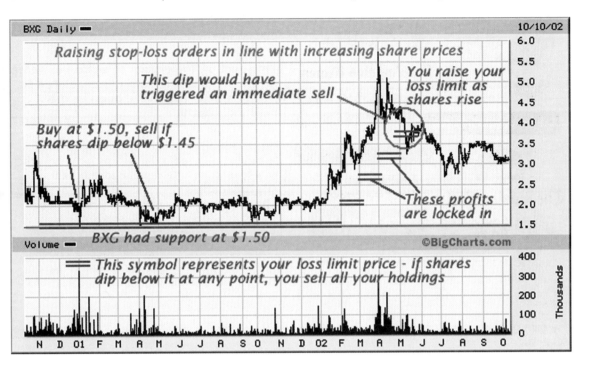

Volatility is a consideration for setting your stop loss price. You do not want to get 'stopped out' which simply means that the price sinks to where your stop order has been set, selling your shares, then immediately rises afterwards, further into profitable territory.

By placing your original stop below the support level you have minimized the chance of getting stopped out at first. However the correct placement of stops gets more complicated once you are following a rising price. Individual investors need to decide on their own stop levels based on the volatility of the underlying stock, the momentum of the share's price trend, and their personal investment style.

The investment methodologies presented here are best suited for investment levels of at least $1500 or more per stock, so that commission costs will be minimal as a percentage of overall investment value.

Chapter Seven: Media Bites

You may have seen my comments in...

...and many others not listed here.

The media has had a lot to say about penny stocks in recent years, and because of my involvement with the industry I have kept an eye on the news.

This section includes a selection of some of the articles and comments related to penny stocks that have been in the media recently.

Personally, I have been interviewed on television and radio, as well as quoted in the newspapers for my revolutionary theories and approaches to investing in penny stocks. I have also written and self-published such books as *Stocks That Will Make You Money*.

In addition, my writing and theories have been incorporated into and displayed upon nearly twenty different financial websites. I am frequently contacted by media organizations for comments, live interviews, and discussions.

My comments and select quotes have been picked up by media sources from North America to Australia.

Barron's Newspaper reviewed PeterLeeds.com in their April 22, 2002 edition. Below are some of their comments.

A brainchild of Peter Leeds, who has written books on penny stocks and provided content to related Websites... It's updated daily, and chock-full of tips for serious small-cap investors.

Leeds's approach works for investors who like to be told what to invest in and why, by someone who has already done the legwork - and who has a credible track record. He makes a weekly pick, for which he provides a full report and links to research data.

Also, Leeds follows up on past picks and general market news. Special articles and reports help you further understand the market as you develop a small-cap strategy. And Leeds's watchlist notes stocks that may yet have potential - just not today.

You can view the individual performance of Leeds' picks at the site; he claims an overall 140% average gain since the service's inception in 1997.

...as for traditional penny stocks traded over the counter, experts say they have always been volatile - and risky - because the companies behind them often are still in their development phases.

"About 95 percent of penny stocks are bad investments," said Peter Leeds, president of PeterLeeds.com, an Internet publication with several thousand subscribers.

Nevertheless, there can be gold in some low-priced stocks - if the investor has patience and a knack for picking companies on the rebound, Leeds said.

For instance, his publication picked USANA Health Sciences as a sure bet for recovery last December when the company's stock was at $1.15.

Its shares closed yesterday at $6.20.

I was asked by the Associated Press to comment on the Enron situation. Below is an excerpt from the interview. (Also see the Enron Case Study in Chapter Five of *Understanding Penny Stocks*).

Peter Leeds, president of PeterLeeds.com and author of "Stocks That Will Make You Money," said penny stocks should be discovered before anyone else recognizes a good deal — not bought on the cheap after falling from lofty heights.

Enron descended into bankruptcy in December amid allegations of accounting abuses that included hidden debt and inflated profits. Shares that approached $90 each in the fall of 2000 plummeted to less than a dollar, leaving workers and retirees with depleted 401(k)s that had been loaded with Enron stock.

Leeds said penny stocks are particularly volatile, and 95 percent of them are poor investments. His company tries to find the 5 percent with realistic upside potential, using criteria that include a proven management team, growing revenues and earnings, a low or nonexistent debt load, patented technologies or innovations, and market dominance.

"I would say that Enron falls well short in all of these categories," Leeds said. "From our perspective this rules out the stock many times over."

He said Enron meets the criteria for high trading volume and brand recognition. But the volume decrease since January makes it more difficult to profit from speculative trading. And the name "has a negative connotation and so is an additional strike against the stock," Leeds said.

Even Enron officials have said they will leave the name behind as it reorganizes to focus on its natural gas pipelines and power operations and tries to emerge from bankruptcy.

When I was interviewed by KPHN live radio about penny stocks, the host of the *Total Business Show*, Scott Simon, asked me to share some of my favorite penny stock success stories. I gladly brought up Bre-X.

While the majority of people have a negative connotation about the stock (the reasons for which are detailed below), I explained that it was actually an excellent investment from the perspective of penny stock investors.

You see, it was the penny stock traders that made excessive profits (and I do mean excessive - hundreds of dollars turned into millions) from the stock, while the more conservative and 'safe' investors were the ones who got so badly burned by getting involved late at high prices.

To read more about this incredible penny stock story, be sure to check out my Bre-X Case Study from Chapter Five.

Chapter Seven:
Watch Out for These Dangers

If you are looking for a service that picks penny stocks for you, or even if you are just trying to get extra information on that investment you have been watching, you should keep the following principles in mind.

Ulterior Motives:

Is your 'source' promoting the stock because they want to help you achieve big returns? Probably not.

In many cases, the publisher of that penny stock report, or the salesperson calling you about the latest hot stock is being motivated by their own profits. They often get compensation from the companies they talk about, and that compensation is often in the form of shares. Thus, if their efforts drive the share prices higher, they are looking at a pretty profit.

To get a better idea of the kind of scams running amok out there, check out the movie, "Boiler Room."

Approximately 75% of the penny stock promoters (whether web pages or printed newsletters or otherwise) have ulterior motives which may be very dangerous to your capital, and the same can be said for over 95% of the services that give the 'advice' away free.

You can protect yourself by asking questions, by reading the disclaimer of each service word by word, and by building a relationship with the people running the service before you even think of following their advice.

In addition, remember that most services manipulate or mis-state their track records, and they are not afraid to lie to you if that means they may make a few bucks.

If you get an opinion from a friend or co-worker you should put some stake in it, but remember at the same time that their experience with the service and the penny stocks they have traded will be different (whether better or worse) than your own.

Your best bet is to go with the penny stock professionals at PeterLeeds.com. I encourage you to visit the web site and decide for yourself if we can meet your needs.

Peter Leeds accepts no compensation from the companies featured, and in nearly every case has no contact whatsoever with them. (Exceptions include when our research team needs clarification from a CEO, for example, but even then we usually utilize an inconspicuous e-mail or pretend to be an interested investor).

When the media is looking for experts in the area of penny stocks, they go to PeterLeeds.com. We have been featured and quoted in CBS MarketWatch, Yahoo! financial news, the Associated Press, News.com.au, the LA Times, and many others, as well as having been interviewed live on television and radio.

Danger List	
Ulterior Motives	Tips at Work
Specific Prices	Message Boards
Professional Analysts That Are Not Really That Professional	

Tips at Work:

No matter how excited your co-worker is about a stock, and no matter how amazing it may sound, when you are hearing a penny stock tip you should instantly become wary.

You may be the ten thousandth person that same information has passed through, and I can almost guarantee that you are not the first, and you are not the second, and you are not the one hundredth. (And that even applies if this tip is from his 'cousin's friend.' It's from everybody's cousin's friend!)

The more urgency you feel to rush out and buy the stock, the more likely it is that others before you have done the same thing. The more incredible the story that the company boasts, the more likely it is false.

Be aware that there are devious forces at work who make a very good living starting penny stock rumors. They plant the idea in the heads of a few of their friends or associates, and the concept spreads.

Even after it has migrated away from the source by passing through two dozen different people in each direction, those that continue to spread the rumor always seem to think that this 'special knowledge' comes from their friend's sister. Or the "brother of a guy at the plant who knows a friend of mine." It doesn't.

While your friends probably have very good intentions, and are honest people, they have fallen victim to a trap that is beyond their control. You can then either add yourself to the casualty list, or protect yourself from the fallout.

Ask Your Friend Any of These Questions.
1. What are the company's revenues?
2. What is their debt load?
3. How many outstanding shares are there?
4. What is the name of the CEO?
5. Who are their competitors?

If your friend can not answer these, you should probably wonder how much he really knows.

(By the way, he or she will probably answer #5. It will go something like this: "They have no competitors! The technology is patented, and it is so revolutionary that they are the only ones who have North American distribution rights...")

This is not to say that you will never be approached with a penny stock tip that could possibly make you some money. Just fight off any impatience you feel to gobble up $50,000 worth, and apply the techniques in the earlier chapters of this book to do your own due diligence.

After that, if you still feel inclined, you can proceed with confidence that you are taking full responsibility for your actions. If the stock tanks after you buy it, you may want to blame your friend, but it is really your own fault.

You should also know that on some occasions you may be able to get involved with one of these promotional companies and make money, despite the fact that it is a terrible operation, or the interest is purely based upon some rumor running rampant. As more and more people buy in, the share price may climb even if there is no justification besides the rumor mill.

If you are getting involved while keeping this in mind, and you are willing to accept the risk, and you think you are buying in early enough, you may be able to turn some profit. However, everyone always thinks that they are in early enough, but they almost never are.

Specific Prices:

If you ever are given specific prices that a stock is supposed to hit, you should immediately feel cautious. We are not talking about becoming a subscriber to PeterLeeds.com and getting their target buy and sell prices that are based on research and calculations. We are talking about the tip you hear where your colleague is saying that, "As soon as ABC gets the patent, the stock is going to hit $7.00!"

Firstly, the $7.00 number does not come from your colleague's research. It comes directly from the mouth of the promoter who started the rumor, because he will be selling at $5.50. He needs to make sure that all of his 'goats' are locked in, waiting for that last price spike while he unloads his shares. Without a target price as bait, profit-takers may erode his efforts before he skips town.

In addition, beyond providing price opinions that are based upon professional research, it is not legal to guarantee, or otherwise imply a guarantee of a future stock price. While some traders are better than others at predicting share price activity, no one can know the prices to which a stock will travel, and if they pretend to, they are either dishonest or naive.

Professional Analysts That Are Not Really That Professional:

It seems that every web page out there is claiming to have professional analysts and research teams. As most of the penny stock web sites are programmed by kids using their parents' computers, it makes me wonder exactly what they mean by 'professional' and 'research team.'

It also makes me feel bad for the innocent web surfers who were snared by this trap. Certainly they had no way of knowing that the claims were false, but it is nearly impossible to encourage regulatory bodies to take any action against these claims. (I may have found a way, so visit our section later in this chapter entitled, The New Sheriff in Town).

If you are going to try one of these other services, despite my continued warnings as well as the shameless promotion of my own service, make sure to test them with questions.

Message Boards:

Never have I seen such a cesspool of mis-information. I highly recommend avoiding them at all costs. In most cases, a message board's activity is made up of a handful of individuals arguing with one another, their positions being driven mainly by whether or not they own shares. And as often as not, their comments are so incorrect or misunderstood that they do more harm than good.

A message board is the tool of the naive. Use the quality research techniques we have described in this book and leave the message boards to the monkeys.

Chapter Seven:
Benefits to Look for in Investment Picking Services

VERY IMPORTANT! Protect yourself.

Any web site or service (even printed) offering free penny stock picks is almost certainly being paid to promote those companies. And the types of companies that need to pay a service to promote their stock are generally pretty lousy!

You may read a glowing report on some company with a miracle, break-through, patented technology, but if their claims were really true they would not need to be paying some tout sheet to give them a glowing review.

There are many different investment picking services out there, so if you have decided to join one of them here is what you need to know:

• Do they offer professional service, or do they just 'say' they offer professional service?

This is easy enough to find out, just by dropping them an e-mail with a question to see how they reply. Better yet, send the exact same question to your top 3 services and compare the speed of response and the quality of response.

Benefits You Deserve
• Professional Service
• Professional Research Team
• Full Team, Not a One-Man-Show
• Learning Experience
• Ongoing Coverage of Past Picks
• Quality, not Quantity
• Media Recognition
• Unsolicited testimonials
• Verifiable Track Record

• Do they have a professional research team, or do they just say they have a professional research team?

We have looked around. Very, very few have a professional research team, they are almost all just one-man (a few two-man) shows. Their backgrounds are not always even in the financial industry! Don't trust your money to someone who treats the business as a hobby.

- **Avoid one-man shows!**

If the site is owned by the same guy doing the stock picks, he will never fire himself regardless of how bad he does. That is a tremendous disadvantage for you. A service like PeterLeeds.com (yes, I am biased) has fired analysts in the past when they were not meeting the stringent performance requirements demanded by management.

- **Look for a learning experience.**

Any 12 year old kid can put out a web site with stock picks nowadays. If you are a new investor, you may want to find a **real** service that will go that much further, providing you with ongoing e-mail guidance, learning articles, and handling your questions as they arise.

- **Beware of "Fire and Forget" newsletters.**

"Fire and Forget" newsletters comprise approximately 85% to 90% of the services out there. They say, "Buy this stock" then you never hear about it again, especially if it does not perform well.

One of the best features of my service is our daily updates. Using new trading and corporate information, we update our site daily to give you the biggest penny stock advantage.

- **Picks! Picks! Picks! Losses! Losses! Losses!**

Many services focus on quantity rather than quality. And, many people naively push the services to do so, wanting to get daily picks, or even several picks per day!

I pulled the following comment from the *cliche closet*: "You are only cheating yourself!" Want 15 picks a week? You are basically pressuring some person of questionable ability to come up with handfuls of ticker symbols, and you are sinking your money into them! This is not a profitable investment approach.

If you do not believe me, please go ahead right now and join a daily stock picking service. When you have come back in a few weeks, wiser and poorer, start reading again from this point.

- **Look for a service recognized by the media.**

Who has been getting the interviews and radio appearances, and quotes in the paper? No service more so than ours , and there is a reason for that.

- **Unsolicited testimonials.**

Unsolicited testimonials from people just like you are a great way to tell how happy people are with the service. The trick, of course, is knowing which are real and which were just made up to pad some guy's marketing. Can you tell which of these are true and which are false?

Which 2 Testimonials are Real?	
A. Although right now I'm just getting the feel of your site without actually investing, in one day I already saw a 30% gain in XYBR. You also called this in an article 3 days ago.	**B.** I had been losing money before getting your help, and since then I have made back

163

All I have to say is WOW! This makes me for the first time feel secure about taking some of your suggestions and investing in your picks. If only I signed up a week earlier. Thanks again and I will be writing to you soon.

☐ Real ☐ Fake

all of my losses, and then some!

☐ Real ☐ Fake

C. I am up over 50% in my portfolio since taking your advice, and all three of the stocks I bought have gone up. Thanks, and keep up the good work.

☐ Real ☐ Fake

D. Since subscribing in June my small portfolio has increased by around 1000% and I did not trade it for two months because of holidays.

☐ Real ☐ Fake

Now, read on to the bottom of this section for the answers!

- **The Truth Behind the Numbers.**

It would be a mistake to base your decision on a track record alone. Firstly, because past performance has little to do with future performance, but you already knew that.

Secondly, many good gain numbers are not applicable, especially those related to OTC stocks, because you probably can't sell them to take the gains anyway. (OTC stocks are easy to buy and very hard to sell, even if they rise in price).

Thirdly, the numbers may be made up or tweaked by the service. Yes, they do this, and you can report such practices to The New Sheriff In Town. (see in the upcoming section)

The real testimonials were **A** and **D**. They were sent to PeterLeeds.com by members of the service.

The point is, it is nearly impossible to tell which are real and which are fake. That is why it is so important to protect yourself when looking into services on the internet or otherwise, especially those that deal with investments. Do not base your decision on testimonials or track record alone, but instead on several factors, such as those described in this article.

Chapter Seven:
Do Your Own Research

The best way to come up with good stock picks is through a combination of professional opinions and your own hard work.

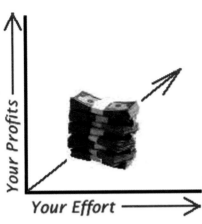

Your Profits / **Your Effort**

Don't invest in something just because the service you joined says to. And don't load all of your hard earned money into a stock that you found on your own, if you do not have a good investment track record in the past.

Even if you decide to get stock picks from a service, you should still do your own research. Look deeply into the companies that the service talks about, and see if you agree or disagree with their findings. Confirm the numbers and details they provide. Ask yourself if this stock meets your own investment objectives, risk tolerance, and timeframe outlook.

Some good ways to do your own research are detailed in this book:

• First, learn Leeds Analysis and apply it to the stocks you are interested in.

• Use the tools and Internet pages described in My Picks for High Quality Web Sites to isolate and research potential investments.

• Have a clear understanding of your investment goals, financial situation, timeframe outlook, and risk tolerance.

• Watch the stocks you like for a while before investing. Even if it goes up and you miss out, you will have learned that your method of coming up with stocks may be effective. And don't worry, because there is always another good stock just around the corner.

You can benefit dramatically by joining a proven penny stock picking service, like PeterLeeds.com. However, you will benefit the most, and learn the greatest amount if you research the shares of each company before you invest, in complement to the *Hot List* penny stock picks that PeterLeeds.com provides.

Chapter Seven:
My Picks for High-Quality Web Sites

Learning: To learn all about penny stocks, trading, and brokers, visit PeterLeeds.com. Also, here are a few of my favorites:

- Investopedia.com
- The Motley Fool (Fool.com)
- StockTradingResources.com

Glossaries: For penny stock terms, I suggest the use of the glossary included in this book. As well, check out these sites:

- InvestorWords.com
- Investopedia

Stock Screeners: Screeners help you build a short-list of stocks based on the parameters you set. For example, a screener could provide you with a list of stocks that trade between $0.25 and $0.35, or that have positive earnings, or that are involved in a specific industry.

I suggest the use of screeners to build short-lists of stocks that you can then apply Leeds Analysis to, in order to uncover the most promising penny stock investments.

For example, you can choose to derive a list of stocks that trade between $1.50 and $1.80, have a positive P/E ratio, and are listed on the NASDAQ SmallCap market. Good screeners allow you to set your preferred range for the price per share, market, revenues, earnings, and industry for the underlying stocks. As well, some enable you to select ranges for average trading volumes, year low or year high, and more advanced fundamental ratios like debt/equity.

- Yahoo! Stock Screener (http://screen.yahoo.com/stocks.html)
- Quicken Stock Search (www.Quicken.com)

Quotes and Charts: I strongly suggest the use of charts when tracking or analyzing your stocks. A picture is worth a thousand words. By far, the best charting service on the Internet is BigCharts, based on ease of use, reliability, speed, and information presentation.

- BigCharts.com - Get quotes and charts at the same time
- Yahoo! Finance Quotes (http://finance.yahoo.com)

Company News: Many services that provide quotes also provide news and press releases.

- BigCharts.com - Recent news releases are included below the charts
- Yahoo! Finance Quotes (http://finance.yahoo.com) - Get a quote, news items are included below quote details

Portfolio Monitor: With a portfolio monitor, you can track several stocks at once. This is very useful in combination with Paper Trading to help you keep an eye on your picks. It is also an effective tool when you want to monitor many potential investments at once, in order to look for trading opportunities.

- Yahoo! Finance Portfolio (http://finance.yahoo.com)

Stock Profiles: Profiles give you a snapshot look at a company, including an explanation of their business model, some select trading data, and some fundamental details. Each profile is different depending on the source, so you may want to get profiles from several different sources for the same stock.

- CBS MarketWatch Profile (http://www.marketwatch.com/tools/quotes/profile.asp?)
- Yahoo! Finance Profile (http://finance.yahoo.com) - Get a quote, then choose 'profile'

Financial News: The television is often a better source of financial news, but the Internet runs a close second. Newspapers and magazines are great, but they are often outdated by the time you are reading them. Here are some good sources of financial news.

- Yahoo! Finance (http://finance.yahoo.com)
- CNNfn.com
- CNBC.com
- BigCharts.com

Message Boards: I discourage the use of message boards, even for those of you who understand the dangers of misinformation. I can not provide any insight into which message boards are the best.

Penny Stock Picks: Before getting any penny stock picks, help yourself by reading the following sections of *Understanding Penny Stocks* which are very important; Watch Out for These Dangers, and Benefits to Look for in a Penny Stock Picking Service. There is only one source of penny stock picks I trust, because I created them. They are PeterLeeds.com and it was their sponsorship which made this free educational book happen.

Chapter Seven:
The New Sheriff in Town

This industry is my bread and butter.

Unfortunately for both you and I, we get hurt by every penny stock shyster, and every dishonest web site.

Here I provide two methods for you to help clean up the industry, and together we can hopefully repair the bad name that penny stocks have gotten over the years.

1. Send me your complaints about improprieties, blatant lies, and even anything that does not seem to jive.

We will investigate every complaint, and will take appropriate action to help clean up this town. This action includes reporting individuals or organizations to the appropriate bodies, compiling documentation and files on the lawless, and even getting legal advice as required.

2. Alternatively, and as is generally a better idea, you could go directly to the authorities yourself. Giving the SEC a quick e-mail legally forces them to look into the complaint.

In either case, you should include your own name and e-mail, a detailed description of the nature of the complaint, and as much pertinent copied and pasted data from their site as you can get your hands on. Remember too, that this does not just apply to web sites, but offline publications as well.

You should also be proud of yourself if you do take such a step, because ultimately it is your own trading backyard that you are cleaning up.

Suspicious of a Service You Have Joined?

Here's what you do:

• Record by printing out every pick they make, as well as every previous pick you have access to, and include the dates.

• Print out a copy of their track record and/or any claims they have made about performance of their service or of specific stocks they have picked.

• Continue adding to your file as they make new picks.

• Do not let them on to the fact that you are doing this. Keep a low profile, and don't blow your cover even if you find something wrong.

• When you have some solid evidence, make a copy of all the information.

• Write a covering letter explaining the situation and send the entire package to the FTC, SEC, or me (E-mail me first if you intend to send me anything).

Chapter Seven:
Old Stock Certificates and Lost Stocks

Old Certificates:

If you want to find out the value of some old share certificates, and you do not mind spending a few dollars, you can call this number and they will do the leg-work for you: (I believe it costs around $60 per certificate)

Stock Certificate Search: (800)537-4523

Or, You Can Do The Work Yourself:

You have a certificate for a company and you'd like to determine if your shares have value. The basic information you will need should all be on the certificate itself, and is as follows:

The name of the company

The date the shares were issued

The state in which the company was incorporated.

Your first goal is to determine the current status of the firm which is likely to be one of the following:

- Still in business (same or different name)
- Acquired or merged with currently operating business
- Not in business / gone bankrupt

The first step would be to see if the company is trading on a listed exchange.

Yahoo.com offers a symbol lookup feature Symbol Lookup which will tell you if the firm is still trading under the same name.

Call or write the transfer agent that is listed on the front of each certificate. A transfer agent handles transfers of stock certificates and should be able to advise you on their value.

If the transfer agent no longer exists or cannot help you, try to contact the company directly. The stock certificates should show the state where the company was incorporated. Contact the Secretary of State in that state, and ask for the Business Corporations Section. They should be able to give you a history of the company. From there you can contact the existing company (if there is one) to find out the value of your stocks.

If the firm no longer exists (in any form) your certificate may have value as a collector's item, but at this point most hope is lost. A site like **www.scripophily.com** is one of the largest dealers of certificates on the internet.

If you don't want to do the research yourself you can always hire one of the many firms on the internet that will research your shares for you.

One Quick Method to Determine if Your Shares Have Value:

You can attempt to deposit your certificates with a brokerage firm. The firm has to determine the value of the shares.

Chapter Eight:
Questions and Answers

I have been in the penny stock business for a long time, and I have always been there to help answer questions.

Over the years literally hundreds of thousands of questions crossed my e-mail account, and do you know what? About 95% of them were the same, common questions, over and over.

This chapter of *Understanding Penny Stocks* has those questions and the answers, and then a few dozen more not-so-common Q+As.

Chapter Eight:
Beginner Level Questions

What are penny stocks?

Strangely, there is no solid definition for penny stocks. As previously described in Chapter Two of *Understanding Penny Stocks*, there are three different criteria that various individuals and organizations use to delineate and define penny stocks, and what is considered a penny stock really depends with whom you are dealing.

1. Price Per Share

2. Market the Equity Trades Upon

3. Market capitalization

Visit chapter one to read the complete definition as described in *Understanding Penny Stocks*.

Do I need a broker to trade penny stocks?

Yes, to trade penny stocks you will need a broker. It is easy to open an account with them, and then it is simply a matter of giving them your buy and sell orders. This can be done online with most discount brokers, which is the method that I highly recommended.

You can read all about stock brokers, and trading penny stocks in Chapter Two.

What is the difference between a discount broker and a full service broker.

We strongly suggest that you use a discount broker, especially if you are trading penny stocks. We have described the major differences in Chapter Two. There is a list of the top-ranked discount brokers for penny stock traders in that section of the book as well.

How do I get a broker?

Hopefully I have made it easier with the section on top-ranked discount brokers for penny stock traders. Once you have settled on the one that best meets your needs, you simply need to open an account. The brokers know that the more painless their sign-up procedure is, the more customers they will attract. You will probably be pleasantly surprised at how simple it is to get started.

Most online discount brokers will allow you to sign up on the Internet, and it should not take very long at all. Just fill out the forms, and make an initial deposit, and you are ready to buy your first penny stocks!

What do I look for in a broker? As a penny stock trader, what should I consider important?

I have examined the topic of brokers in detail in *Understanding Penny Stocks*, and you can read all about them in the following sections of Chapter Two: **Getting a Good Stock Broker**, and **Where to Research Stock Brokers**.

Can I learn about penny stocks without risking my money?

Absolutely, and I encourage starting off risk-free. Too many investors dive in head first, then have nothing left once they have learned the game. I have included a detailed look at Paper Trading in Chapter Two of this book, which allows you to learn all about trading penny stocks without risking a dime.

What is paper trading and how do I do it?

Review our full discussion on **Paper Trading** in Chapter Two.

Where can I get quotes, charts, and news releases for the penny stocks I am interested in?

We have a detailed examination of the best places to get information on your favorite penny stocks in Chapter Seven, **Information Sources**.

How much time do I need to monitor my investments and research new stocks?

and, How long does it take for penny stocks to show significant gains?

I have seen penny stocks make moves of 300% in one day, and others languish for years without a volatility of more than 40%. It depends on the penny stock in question, the driving factors (like the state of the market, investor sentiment, and sector influences), and your own opinion of the types of gains you would consider significant.

Leeds Analysis uses a review of the state of the market, investor sentiment, and sector influences in its research to pick the best penny stocks for its subscribers of PeterLeeds.com. These, along with all of the other factors (insider trading, shifts in social trends), are combined with their proprietary fundamental and technical analysis strategies to uncover the best penny stock picks for their subscribers. You may want to go to PeterLeeds.com and see what picks they have waiting for you.

How do I buy penny stocks?

This is described in detail in Chapter Two, in the section entitled **Buying Penny Stocks**.

How do I sell penny stocks?

This is described in detail in Chapter Two, in the section entitled **Selling Penny Stocks**.

What is a market order?

Market orders are explained in Chapter Two, in the section **Trading Stocks**.

What is a limit order?

Limit orders are explained in Chapter Two, in the section **Trading Stocks**.

What type of investors are penny stocks most suited for?

I have looked into this topic in the section entitled **Why Trade Penny Stocks**, and have even included a suitability quiz.

Where do penny stocks trade?

I have dedicated an entire section of *Understanding Penny Stocks* to this question, and have titled the section (very appropriately I would say), **Where Do Penny Stocks Trade**?

What is the minimum amount of money required to start trading penny stocks?

You would probably be surprised how often I am asked this question. I usually field this same query about ten to fifteen times a week.

The short answer is zero! You can start trading penny stocks with no money at all, and learn the ropes all at the same time by starting with our paper trading strategies.

When you decide to make that jump to real money, here is what you need to know: The minimum depends entirely on the broker you select. They may require that you make a minimum deposit to open an account (ie-$1,000, $500), while others will let you open an account with no money at all.

Sometimes brokers also have minimum amount per order (ie- $500 per buy transaction minimum or else they won't process it, or they may charge you a huge commission), but that is rare.

When you are ready to put real capital into the penny stock markets, you need to decide how much you want to invest. We suggest, mainly to keep the effect of brokerage commissions down to a small percentage of the total, to invest anywhere from $500 to $1,500 per penny stock. This keeps your exposure to each stock low, and allows for diversification even if you only have a few thousand. (If you get a $20 commission to buy $30 worth of stock, it will not be worth your time and energy, especially as you consider you will take another commission to sell. Your $30 of stock would need to go to $70 just to cover the commissions! Make sure to invest enough to minimize the effect of commissions).

In our opinion, more experienced traders that have larger portfolios at their disposal can go as high as $5,000 per penny stock, but that is a personal decision that should be based on your own investment objectives, sensitivity to risk, and trading aggression.

Chapter Eight:
Intermediate Level Questions

Can penny stocks give me short-term trading profits?

Absolutely. penny stocks by their very nature are highly volatile investments, and are usually very speculative.

This means that they can return gains of hundreds or even thousands of percentage points, while you may only see returns of 5% or 10% in more conventional blue chip stocks over the same period. They also inherently contain more risk.

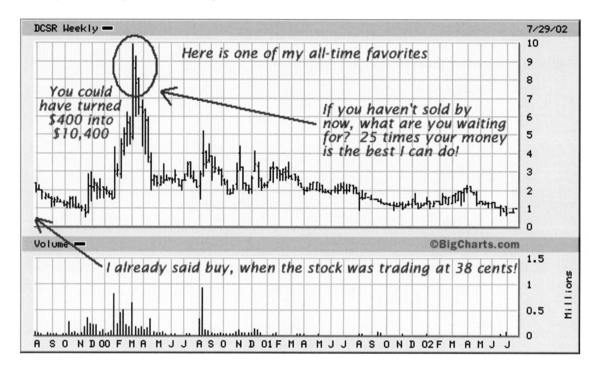

How can I research companies that I am interested in?

I have dedicated Chapter Seven of *Understanding Penny Stocks* solely to revealing the various (and best) sources of information for penny stock investors.

Penny stocks are generally more difficult to research due to a lack of visibility, and it gets worse if they are not traded on a regulated exchange like the NASDAQ. However, as you will see in Chapter Seven, there are all sorts of information sources.

I also highly encourage you to apply our long-secretive Leeds Analysis methods to any stocks you are interested in. The fundamental and technical analysis techniques have been kept to ourselves until being revealed in *Understanding Penny Stocks*, are examined in detail in Chapter Three, **Picking Penny Stocks**.

Should I buy that stock I heard about at work? It sounds promising!

I highly discourage using 'tips' from friends and co-workers as a basis for coming up with penny stocks to invest in.

I know that the particular stock sounds amazing, and I know that you feel you had better not wait too long, or you will miss the boat. Just please do yourself this one favor first: review our section in Chapter Seven entitled, **Watch Out for These Dangers**.

You will then understand why you should steer away from these types of penny stocks, at least unless they pass a serious fundamental screening like Leeds Analysis detailed in Chapter Three, **Picking Penny Stocks**.

How much should I invest in one penny stock?

While that depends on your own financial position, your tolerance to risk, and your own trading aggression, we feel that levels of $1,000 to $1,500, or even as high as $2,000 per stock is most appropriate. This effectively makes the commissions only a small factor in the total trade. As well, it helps you avoid driving up the price yourself if your buying volume is high.

You need to diversify over several penny stocks if possible, even if this is at the expense of your total investment per stock. A trader with $1,500 total may want to buy two or three different penny stocks, while a trader with $5,000 may also only want to buy three penny stocks. Both of these traders will be diversified.

How many penny stocks should I hold at one time?

The more the better. You will benefit from diversity if you spread your invested capital around several stocks. However, it will depend a lot on your own trading philosophy. What is best for one person is not best for another.

As long as you are using money you are willing to risk, and you are not putting too much money into any one penny stock, you should hold as many different companies as you feel comfortable with.

A trader with $1,500 for penny stock trading may buy two or three different companies, while a trader with $5,000 may also buy two or three companies, but would also have the option of diversifying among five or eight, or maybe even more.

In all cases, it is best to keep some cash on the sidelines. Having $3,000 to invest does not mean you have to put all of it into penny stocks right now. Watch the activity of your favorites, and accumulate positions in them when they reach your target buying prices. If buying opportunities do not present themselves, watch and wait. There is no rush, and the next great penny stock opportunity is always just around the corner.

As long as you have some cash on the sidelines you will be able to take advantage of buying opportunities as they arise.

Should I go short-term or long-term?

It really depends on the penny stock, but in many cases it is best to go short-term.

In some cases it is prudent to hold penny stocks for longer time frames, and as much as several years. This would apply to companies that are solid, and have legitimate prospects, and just need some time to demonstrate the effectiveness of their operational strategy and business plan.

The important thing to remember is that you should not be holding a penny stock just because you are frustrated with it, or because it has fallen below what you bought it at, or because it has not done much yet.

Before you get involved with shares in a company have a clear idea of how long you would intend to hold the shares and why. If the stock has not performed as you would expect in that time you should take another look at the situation, and perhaps move on to other investments.

How do I check out a company to make sure it is legit?

Legitimacy is not the problem. It is the legitimate companies that are so poorly run, or are based on a faulty business plan, which will cost you 100% of your investment as they tank. You will lose just as much with these as with some made-up promotional scheme.

Checking out the legitimacy of a company is a lot easier with penny stocks that are trading on the AMEX or the NASDAQ (or the Canadian exchanges like the TSX or TSX-Venture), than it is for Over-The-Counter and pink sheets stocks.

OTC companies are not subject to very significant reporting requirements, or any official form filings that would prove their legitimacy. Pink sheet stocks are even worse.

Organizations like the Better Business Bureau are of little help, because illegitimate companies can easily change their name from time to time as cover, and the BBB is generally a powerless organization to begin with.

You should also be wary of the company web sites, because there is no method of telling fact from fiction when you are on their page.

The best approach involves a combination of phoning the company, e-mailing their investor relations contact, and reading the press releases. As well, make sure to review any documents filed with the SEC (Securities and Exchange Commission).

We suggest limiting your penny stock investments to those shares trading on the NASDAQ SmallCap and the AMEX. That way you will not need to worry about the legitimacy of these corporations. The exchanges have already done the job for you, before granting listing approval.

Why wasn't my trade order filled?

With all specific trading questions you should first go directly to your broker. As well, you can get even further details to the explanation below in Chapter Two of *Understanding Penny Stocks*, in the section on **Trading Stocks**.

If your order was not filled (or was only partially filled), your limit price may not have been high enough (or low enough if you were selling) to match any traders on the other side of the deal. In other words, I can put in an order to buy IBM shares at $1.00, but the order will not get filled because I am not paying enough.

If your limit price was reached during trading, but you still did not get the shares, you need to remember that the exchange takes orders as first come, first served priority. For example, if someone puts 10,000 shares for sale at $1.10, then afterwards you put 2,000 for sale at the same price ($1.10), your shares are 10,000 deep. Even if buyers meet the $1.10 price, they would need to gobble up 12,000 shares for your order to be fully filled. If they only took on 4,000 there would still be another 6,000 ahead of you, and then your 2,000.

In this example, if 11,000 shares were bought at $1.10, that would leave you with a partial fill: 1,000 sold at your asking price, and 1,000 did not so you still own them.

Why does this penny stock show no trades or volume?

Often a penny stock will go the full day (or several days) without the bid and ask prices meeting up, which means no trades take place. This is usually more common with very thinly traded penny stocks. If there is not enough investor interest, and those traders that do get involved can not agree upon a price, there will be no activity in the underlying stock.

Chapter Eight:
Advanced Level Questions

Should I average down?

If you review my explanation of averaging down in Chapter Four, and the discussion of it, you will see that I do not suggest averaging down. Instead, I am a bigger supporter of 'averaging up,' where you buy into strength as a stock gains momentum.

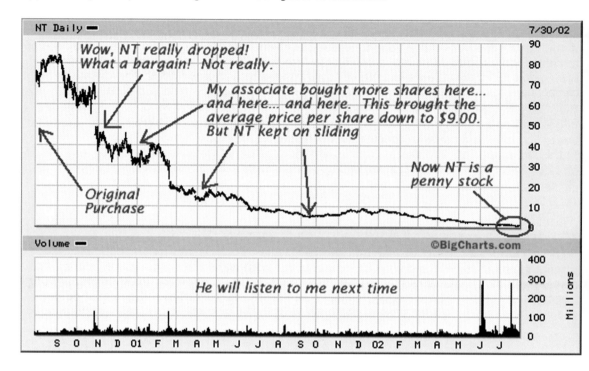

How do I pick winning penny stocks myself?

Earlier in *Understanding Penny Stocks*, I have revealed Leeds Analysis, which is the ultimate penny stock selection method. It takes up nearly all of Chapter Three.

I have a specific penny stock I am interested in buying. Where can I get an opinion?

It is against my policy to comment on the suitability of investments beyond the scope of our published positions. This is for several different reasons, including legal considerations. As well, I would not be inclined to (or have the time to) look deeply enough into the company to make what I feel would be a proper comment.

Your best bet is to do a little research yourself, applying Leeds Analysis which I have revealed earlier in *Understanding Penny Stocks*.

What external factors impact the penny stock markets?

All of the same driving factors that influence the broader exchanges (like government policy, interest rate moves, the price of oil, political uncertainty...) also have an effect on penny stock shares.

The difference is that smaller penny stock companies usually feel the effects to a magnified extent, because it does not take much trading volume to throw the stock around.

One external factor that impacts penny stocks specifically, beyond those touched on above, include social perceptions towards the risk/reward ratio of these speculative investments. When traders are reminded by the media that Microsoft used to be a penny stock, they are reminded of the potential gains, and flock towards penny stocks to take their chance. When they hear of an old widow milked out of her life's savings by some hustler, they withdraw from the penny stock scene.

In general, as a bull market progresses and stocks perform better and better, more investors are willing to take a risk with speculative penny stocks.

After a market crash, or in a bear market, investors tend to look for safety and security, and so are more likely to pull out of and stay clear of penny stocks.

Why can I not sell short or buy on margin?

Most brokers only provide 'option eligible' services to stocks trading above $5.00. If a stock is option eligible, it can be sold short or bought on margin. If not, as is the case with penny stocks, you can't. In other words, brokers do not like traders to get fancy with speculative investments.

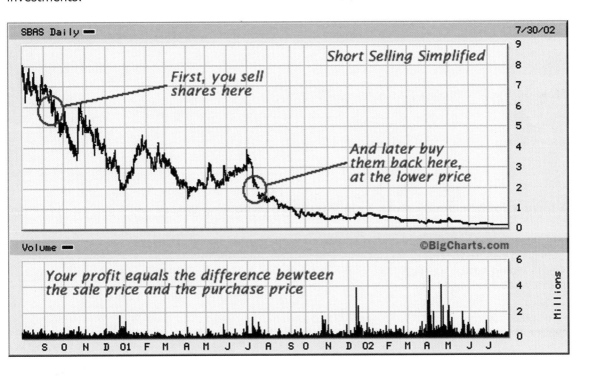

Be sure to take a look at my earlier comments on short selling from Chapter Four, **Advanced Strategies**.

What is technical analysis?

Review my complete discussion of technical analysis in Chapter Three, starting with the section **Different Schools of Thought**.

What is fundamental analysis?

Review my complete discussion of fundamental analysis in Chapter Three, starting with the section **Different Schools of Thought**.

How do I know when to buy a penny stock?

How do I know what price to buy a penny stock at?

How do I know when to sell a penny stock?

How do I know what price to sell my penny stocks at?

I suggest using the specific Leeds Analysis techniques revealed in Chapter Three to uncover what are the best buy and sell prices and times.

Chapter Eight:
Miscellaneous Questions

How can I find out if my old stock certificates have any value?

To address this specific question I have included a full section on this in Chapter Seven, entitled, **Old Stock Certificates**.

I own some stock certificates. Can I transfer these to my broker?

Certainly, assuming that the companies still have any trading value. Your broker can explain how to transfer the stocks over to them, after which you will be able to trade the shares.

Which penny stock picking services can I trust?

There are hundreds if not thousands of stock picking services out there, and we are sad to say that most of them are dishonest, misleading, or ineffective. The majority take compensation from the companies they promote.

Make sure to ask the questions that I have provided in the Chapter Seven section, **Benefits to Look for in a Penny Stock Picking Service.**

As well, read the Chapter Seven discussion on Watch Out for these Dangers.

Of course, I am supporting the services of PeterLeeds.com, a company with which I am closely affiliated, and which is the sole sponsor of this book. PeterLeeds.com does not receive any form of compensation from the companies they research, and their picks have done so well that they have quickly become the predominant service for penny stock picks.

I suggest deciding for yourself after some comparison. Hopefully you will at least visit PeterLeeds.com to get an idea of what we offer.

Can I buy shares directly from the company?

It is possible, but we strongly discourage this practice as is described in Chapter Two, **Where Do Penny Stocks Trade**?

Should I invest in Canadian penny stocks?

It depends on your trading objectives and style.

Certainly there are many more penny stocks trading on regulated exchanges in Canada, so you benefit from a greater choice and a higher standard of reporting requirements.

At the same time, you will be subject to higher commissions from your broker and may not have access to the same information that is available for U.S. based penny stocks.

Certainly there are a great deal of Canadian penny stocks to choose from, but if you are not able to find the best penny stocks to invest in among the U.S. markets, what makes you think that you will be able to do so on foreign exchanges?

Should I invest in international penny stocks?

Again, this depends on your own motivations and objectives. We do not see any need for U.S. investors to look overseas for penny stocks, unless they have some compelling reason to do so.

Why does a stock get halted, and what does it mean?

A stock can be halted either voluntarily by the company itself, if they have some significant news to release that may impact the share price, or by the parent exchange due to negative reasons like failing to provide required data to the exchange, or failure to meet listing requirements.

When a stock is halted you will be unable to trade shares. Often, if the halt is for the release and dissemination of a news item, the stock will start trading again at a different price (higher or lower accordingly) than it was at when trading was interrupted. Stocks can stay halted for a matter of hours, or for several days. In some cases, especially if the news is very bad, the stock may remain halted for weeks, or never resume trading at all.

You can review my explanation of halted stocks in the bonus section of *Understanding Penny Stocks*.

Chapter Nine:
Glossary of Terms

Ask: The price at which selling investors are willing to sell their shares to buyers. You can learn all about ask prices and trading penny stocks in Chapter Three.

Averaging Down: Buying more shares of a stock you already own, and getting the new shares at a lower price because the stock has been dropping. There is a complete discussion of Averaging Down in Chapter Four.

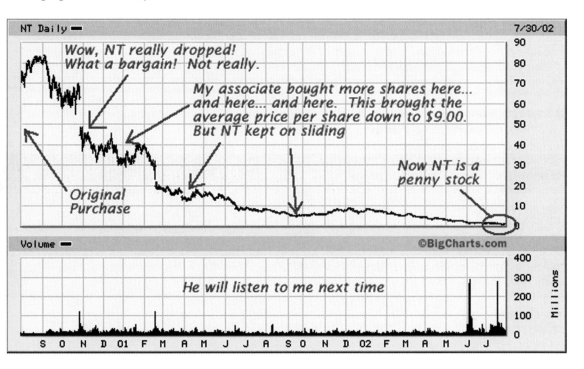

Blue Chip Stocks: Companies that are considered safe and conservative investments, with low downside risk. These stocks are widely held, have major market capitalizations, and have a certain degree of price stability. Companies like Ford, General Electric, and IBM are considered Blue Chip stocks. For a detailed explanation of the differences between Blue Chip and penny stocks, read Big Stocks vs. Penny Stocks in Chapter Two.

Bid: The price that buying investors are willing to pay for shares of stock.

Delistings: When a stock ceases to be traded by a stock exchange it is considered delisted. There are various reasons a stock would get delisted, such as failure to meet the parent exchange's listing requirements, movement to another exchange, or being taken over by another company. There is a portion of *Understanding Penny Stocks* on this topic, entitled **Halts and Delistings**, which can be found in the bonus section of the book.

Duration of Trade Order: The amount of time you want a trade order to be active for. When you enter a buy or sell order, it can be 'good till close' (it will expire at the end of the day, whether filled or not), or good until a certain date you set (ie- good until friday, 18th). Orders expire at the end of the trading day unless you have set a longer duration. You can read more about this in Chapter Two.

Fundamental Analysis: A method of researching a stock that looks at fundamental factors, which include; financial results, financial ratios, industry conditions, press releases, and more. For a full discussion of fundamental analysis, and details about how we use it to pick winning penny stocks, please see **Different Schools of Thought** and **Leeds Analysis** in Chapter Three.

Leeds Analysis: We have developed Leeds Analysis over many years, and reveal full details about it for the first time ever in Chapter Three of *Understanding Penny Stocks*. It is a method of combining fundamental and technical analysis to uncover the best penny stocks to invest in, and isolate the most advantageous prices to trade the stock.

Halts: When an exchange temporarily (or sometimes permanently) stops a stock from trading. In some cases, the company can request that their own stock be halted. Causes for halts are numerous, but usually involve the release of significant information that will have an impact on the share price. The halt allows for sufficient time for the news or announcement to disseminate through the shareholders. You can review the section on **Halts and Delistings** in Chapter Ten.

Hedging: Diversifying exposure or managing risk through opposing investments. For a more involved explanation, visit **Hedging** in Chapter Four.

Examples of Hedging	
In this situation:	**You could hedge by:**
You are concerned about the future of a company in which you hold shares	Buy stock in a direct competitor
Your transport stock shares always do poorly when fuel prices increase	Take up a position in an oil production company
Your biotech shares are a long-shot: They are looking for a cure for breast cancer	If they are not successful, buying stock in a breast cancer treatment company will help cover the bases. If the biotech company is successful, their stock increase will far outweigh any losses you took on the treatment stock, whose shares would slump once the cure was verified

Large Cap Stocks: The 'Cap' refers to capitalization (number of shares times price per share = company capitalization). Large capitalization stocks are worth hundreds of millions of dollars, as opposed to small cap stocks, which may only be worth $50 million or less.

Limit Orders: You want to buy or sell shares of a stock, and have specified the exact price you are willing to accept per share. A full discussion of limit orders can be found in Chapter Two.

Market Capitalization: The number of shares of a company times the price per share = the market capitalization. It is a method of quickly calculating a company's 'worth.' For example, ABC with 1 million outstanding shares at $2 each has a market cap of $2 million. If those shares dropped to $1.50, the market cap would drop to $1.5 million.

Market Orders: You want to buy or sell shares of a stock without providing a price per share that you are willing to accept. You will get the best available price at the time your order reaches the market. A full discussion of market orders can be found in Chapter Two.

NASDAQ: Here is a description of this stock market straight from the horse's mouth: "As the world's largest electronic stock market, NASDAQ® is not limited to one central trading location. Rather, trading is executed through NASDAQ's sophisticated computer and telecommunications network, which transmits real-time quote and trade data to more than 1.3 million users in 83 countries. Without size limitations or geographical boundaries, NASDAQ's "open architecture" market structure allows a virtually unlimited number of participants to trade in a company's stock."

NASDAQ SmallCap: A sub-section of the NASDAQ (above), companies with smaller capitalizations or that can not meet the listing requirements of the main NASDAQ exchange, trade upon the Small Cap. Most stocks on the NASDAQ Small Cap are priced at $1.00 to $5.00 per share.

OTC (Over The Counter): Over-The-Counter stocks refers to any issue that is not traded on a regulated exchange. You can review our full explanation of OTC stocks in our section, **Where Do Penny Stocks Trade**, in Chapter Two.

OTC-BB (Over The Counter Bulletin Board): A regulated quotation service that displays real-time quotes, last-sale prices, and volume information in over-the-counter (OTC) equity securities. An OTC-BB equity security generally is any equity that is not listed or traded on NASDAQ or a national securities exchange. OTC-BB securities include national, regional, and foreign equity issues, warrants, units, American Depository Receipts (ADRs), and Direct Participation Programs (DPPs). In other words, it is a system for creating some regulation and accountability for stocks "without a home." You can review my full explanation of OTC-BB stocks in the Chapter Two section, **Where Do Penny Stocks Trade**.

Paper Trading: Keeping track of imaginary money in real investments, so that you can see how you would have done if you had actually traded. I have provided a complete section on **Paper Trading** in Chapter Two.

Partial Fill: When you trade only a portion of the shares you had intended. For example, you want to buy 4,000 shares of ABC, but at the end of the day have only acquired 1,500. You will still take a full commission charge from your broker for a partial fill.

Penny Stocks: For the purposes of *Understanding Penny Stocks*, I treat any share that trades under $2.00 as a penny stock. However, there is a full section on **What Are Penny Stocks**, in Chapter Two.

Pink Sheets: The pink sheets are stocks that trade without any reporting requirements or regulation, and have no responsibility to you, the investor. They are very hard to buy and sell, as the trading activity in them is very low and sporadic. You can read all about pink sheet stocks in Chapter Two.

Risk Tolerance: The amount of uncertainty/speculation you are willing to accept with your investments. If you are prepared to lose your money but want to try and reap some massive returns, you have a high risk tolerance. If you lay awake at night worried about your $50 investment, you have a low risk tolerance.

Short-Selling: Short selling is the strategy of selling the shares first, then having the commitment to buy them back at a later date. We have an entire section on **Short Selling** in Chapter Four.

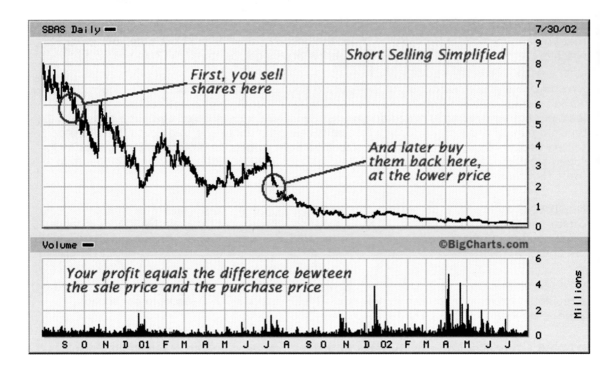

SBAS Daily ■   7/30/02

Short Selling Simplified

First, you sell shares here

And later buy them back here, at the lower price

©BigCharts.com

Volume ■

Your profit equals the difference bewteen the sale price and the purchase price

Small Cap Stocks: The 'Cap' refers to capitalization (number of shares times price per share = company capitalization). Small capitalization stocks are worth a few million dollars, or perhaps as much as $50 million dollars, as opposed to large cap stocks, which may be worth hundreds of millions.

Speculation: The aspect of investing whereby you take a chance or a gamble on a stock. The company may not have much value, and will probably become worthless, but if they strike gold, get that FDA approval, or discover a cure for AIDS, they could explode hundreds of times over in price. Many penny stocks are speculative investments because they are focused on an "all or nothing" result, such as a new biotech drug that may or may not work. Buying into the stock and hoping the drug ends up working is speculation.

Spread: The difference between the bid price and the ask price. You can learn all about bid, ask, and spread starting with the section entitled, **Trading Stocks** in Chapter Two.

Stock Screening: Filtering a list of stocks down into a smaller list based on your parameters. For example, there are thousands of stocks on the NASDAQ, but you could screen these down to all those shares under $2.00, that are profitable, and that are within 10% of their year low. Your shortened list may have only a few dozens stocks. Stock Screening is a great way to pull up a list of potential investments to apply Leeds Analysis to, in order to reveal the best penny stock investment. You can get a review of my favorite web tools, including the best stock screeners, in Chapter Seven.

Takeover: When one company buys out the shares of another, with the purpose being to acquire and run the other. Many penny stocks and their share prices benefit when they are acquired or taken over by a larger firm.

Technical Analysis: A method of stock research that looks at patterns on the trading chart in an attempt to predict future prices. As I explain in *Understanding Penny Stocks*, I suggest that you use technical analysis methods in Leeds Analysis to discover the best prices at which to buy and sell penny stocks.

Ticker Symbol: The letter combination that represents a particular stock. For the purposes of trading and researching stocks, you need to know the company's unique ticker symbol. For example, General Electric trades under the ticker symbol 'GE', while Paravant Computers trades under the ticker symbol 'PVAT.'

Volatility Play Investing: A method of trading stocks that myself and my team have developed. It involves buying and selling the same stocks, again and again, as they undergo repetitive fluctuation in price. You can learn all about **Volatility Play Investing** in Chapter Four.

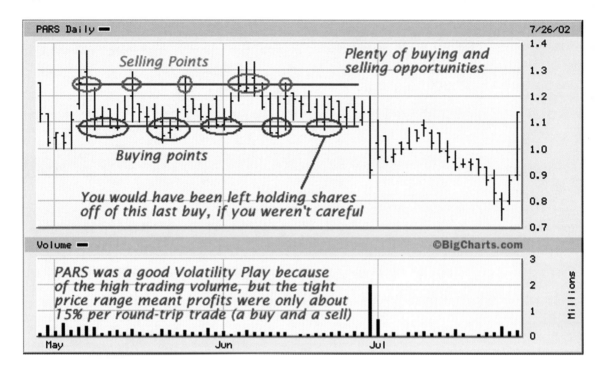

Volume: The number of shares that trade hands per day.

Bonus Chapter:
Penny Stocks Stats Pack

Age of Penny Stock Traders

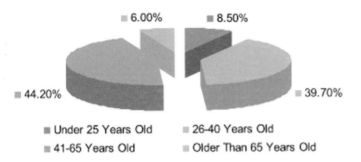

- 6.00%
- 8.50%
- 44.20%
- 39.70%

- Under 25 Years Old
- 26-40 Years Old
- 41-65 Years Old
- Older Than 65 Years Old

Percentage of penny stock web sites that take compensation from the companies they profile: **75%**

Percentage of FREE penny stock web sites that take compensation from the companies they profile: **95%**

Average time for one of PeterLeeds.com's Hot List picks to make a significant (+30%) move: **6 Months**

Fastest gain of greater than 50%: **Same Day** as Hot List pick released

Biggest one-day gain: **235%**

Biggest one-hour gain: **235%**

Track record average: **140%** average, profile price to subsequent high

Household income of Penny Stock Traders (in thousands)

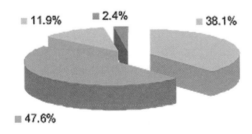

- 11.9%
- 2.4%
- 38.1%
- 47.6%

- Under $50
- $50-$100
- $100-$175
- More than $175

Bonus Chapter:
10 Penny Stock Myths

1. Myth: Blue-Chip stocks are 'safe' investments.

Enron, Bre-X, WorldCom, and Anderson Consulting were all Blue-Chips at one point in their life cycle, before dropping towards or close to $0.

Other blue-chip stocks like Microsoft saw losses from their high of $120 that brought the shares down to $40, for a loss of two-thirds of the total value in about 1 year's time. Blue-chips are plenty dangerous.

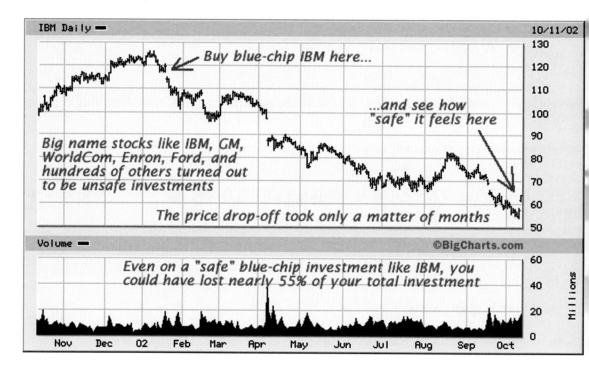

2. Myth: Over time, stocks return strong gains.

This is true if you look back many, many years and compare the level of the overall exchanges to current prices. However, in that time the stocks that make up the indexes have been shuffled, with poor performers being removed in exchange for companies that have seen tremendous growth.

As well, if you do not have the patience to hold on to shares for 50 years, and instead hold on for a ten year window, history shows that you may or may not see significant gains, depending on when you first invested.

3. Myth: To achieve greater returns, you need to assume greater risk.

This is an over-simplified take on the risk-reward ratio. It is possible, using certain investment methodologies such as Leeds Analysis, to lower your risk, while limiting your investments to those with high potential.

4. Myth: Investing with the crowd will be an effective strategy.

The Internet bubble that burst in April of 2000 is a great example of investing with the crowd. The majority of investors got burned (and burned badly) by the collapse that followed, which saw the NASDAQ fall from over 5,000 to lows of 1,300.

5. Myth: You need to pick the bottoms and tops of stocks to make the big profits.

Warren Buffet, the great investor, once said, "Give everybody else the top 5% and the bottom 5%. I'll take everything that's left in between."

Picking bottoms and tops has proven to be impossible, even for 'experts' and market gurus. In your attempt to capture stocks at their absolute lows, you may end up costing yourself much more than if you had just got involved in a stock's trend on the way up.

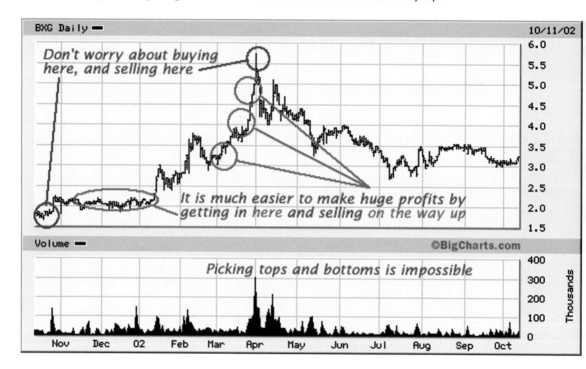

6. Myth: The old rules don't apply to the new economy.

This could not be more wrong. Every time a speculative bubble builds up, people dismiss the fears of others by explaining that, "It's different this time because..." "The stock market CAN continue to climb endlessly, because..."

They cite things like, "New economic policy," "technology creating totally efficient markets," and other things they don't really understand, to justify their unwary approach to greed. And just like it has a dozen times in recent history, it always ends the same way.

7. Myth: Boring companies make for boring returns.

In some cases, sure. But often 'boring' companies, like oil producers, waste disposal companies, and agricultural services, as three examples, are overlooked by investors because of their mundane nature. When these companies then begin to turn huge profits and the street can not ignore them any longer, they can be incredibly rewarding to own.

8. Myth: The Company will do very well because it is in a growing field.

In many cases, a growing industry or field simply gives rise to more competitors. If the number of people entering old age homes per month doubled or tripled, there would be an increase in companies offering locations/accommodations, as much as there would be an increase in business for existing players in the sector.

9. Myth: Stock brokers know the best stocks to invest in.

They often have very educated, and very good opinions, but they do not know the best stocks to invest in just because they are in the field of investing. Stock brokers make a living facilitating transactions - their job is administrative, not analytical.

10. Myth: The company has a good technology that is in great demand, so their share prices will rise.

If the technology is already well-known, as is the potential for the company, the shares may have already swelled in price. If it seems obvious that the company will do well, you may pay too much for shares, especially if you are not getting involved early, before the rest of the investment world.

As well, it takes a lot more than a good technology or idea to make a company run, and subsequently to build shareholder value.

Thomas Edison, the great inventor, once said, "An idea is 1%, hard work makes up the other 99%.

Bonus Chapter:
Financial Statements

Financial statements are a useful tool for judging the health of a company, and for comparing it to its competitors.

They show what the company owes and owns, the profits or losses it has made over a given period, and how their position has changed since their last statement.

Generally if you can tell which direction a company is heading in, you can also forecast future stock prices with some accuracy.

Gaining a basic knowledge of financial statements, and applying this knowledge when choosing or assessing investments can help you pick tomorrow's winning stocks, while avoiding tomorrow's losers.

Of course, financial statement analysis will not forecast future events and unexpected situations which may influence share prices, but it provides a starting point from which to gauge the present value of shares.

Although the topic can get much deeper and more complex, this section of *Understanding Penny Stocks* is designed to give you the ability to understand the numbers and implications of the statements. This knowledge should assist you to make better decisions when doing your due diligence.

Balance Sheet:

The balance sheet shows a company's financial position at a specific date.

One part of the balance sheet shows what the company owns and has owing to it, called assets.

The other part represents liabilities, which are what the company owes. The liabilities also include shareholders' equity, which represents the excess of the company's assets over its liabilities. Shareholder's equity is often referred to as book value.

ASSETS *(What the company owns)*

	Recent Year:	Previous Year:
Current assets:		
Cash and cash equivalents	$ 2,666	$ 4,091
Short-term investments	636	—
Accounts receivable, net	6,685	6,998
Inventories	2,008	2,005
Deferred income taxes	1,460	1,602
Other assets	394	471
Total current assets	13,849	15,167
Property, plant and equipment, net	3,249	2,902
Other assets, net	10,179	4,982
Total assets = current and long-term assets:	$27,277	$23,051

Notice cash levels dropped $1.4 million from one year to the next

LIABILITIES AND STOCKHOLDERS' EQUITY
(What the company owes to others)

	Recent Year:	Previous Year:
Current liabilities:		
Short-term borrowings	$ 453	$ —
Accounts payable	4,380	4,237
Deferred income	972	845
Accrued restructuring costs	1,002	1,110
Other current liabilities	5,031	4,541
Total current liabilities	11,838	10,733

These numbers are usually in thousands (ie- $2,666 means 2.6 million)

Total assets are equal to the sum of the company's liabilities plus the shareholders' equity. In other words, take away liabilities from assets and the remainder is what value is owned by the shareholders.

The Balance Sheet can be used to uncover the value of the company, the debt load, and cash position.

Earnings Statement:

Also called the Income Statement or Profit and Loss Statement, it shows how much revenue a company received during the year from the sale of its products and services, and the expenses the company incurred due to wages, taxes, operating costs, etc...

The difference between revenues and costs is the company's profit or loss for the year.

Continuing Operations:		Recent Year:	Previous Year:
Income			
Net sales	*1. Sales were flat, year over year...*	$ 94,362	$ 94,586
Other		119	388
		94,481	94,974
Costs and Expenses			
Cost of sales (including a $2,000 charge for the discontinuance of a product line in 1997)		73,981	71,561
Selling, general and administrative		13,785	15,631
Research and development	*Numbers in brackets*	2,079	1,002
Litigation settlement income	*are negatives (losses)*	(2,900)	–
Postretirement health care curtailment gain		–	(7,120)
	2. But, expenses increased...	86,945	81,074
Operating Earnings	*3. Which bit into operating earnings*	7,536	13,900
Non-operating Income (Expense)			
Interest income		1,838	1,427
Interest expense		(2,297)	(2,193)
Other, net		(50)	(66)
		(509)	(832)
Earnings before Federal income taxes		7,027	13,068
Federal income tax expense		–	–
Earnings from Continuing Operations		7,027	13,068
Discontinued Operations:			
Loss from operations of discontinued energy business		–	(1,637)
Loss from discontinuance, including provision of $2,000 for operating losses during phase out period		–	(7,000)
Loss from Discontinued Operations		–	(8,637)
Net Earnings		7,027	4,431
Dividends on preferred shares		1,127	1,179
Net Earnings Available for Common Shares		$ 5,900	$ 3,252
Earnings (Loss) Per Common Share:			
Basic:			
Continuing operations		$ 0.94	$ 1.99
Discontinued operations		–	(1.45)
Net Earnings		$ 0.94	$ 0.54
Diluted:	*Here is the important number - net*		
Continuing operations	*earnings doubled year over year,*	$ 0.81	$ 1.67
Discontinued operations	*which is a tremendous result*	–	(1.21)
Net Earnings		$ 0.81	$ 0.46

Net earnings reveal how much money the company 'really' made over the course of the year. Some companies can have low earnings if they used much of their money for research and development, to acquire other companies, fuel aggressive growth, move into new markets, etc...

Some companies have low or negative earnings because they did not generate enough revenues to cover their expenses, or their costs were too high, etc... Be careful of these companies.

Statements of Changes in Financial Position:

This shows how the company's financial position changed from one year to the next. Also called the cash flow statement, this details how the company generated and spent its cash during the year.

This statement can be used in evaluating the liquidity and solvency of a company, and to assess the ability of that company to generate cash internally, to repay debts, to reinvest in itself, etc...

Sources of Financial Reports:

Certainly you can get financials from the companies themselves. Most will gladly fax them to you, or mail you their latest quarterly and annual reports.

However, a faster way to access the information can be by Internet.

For example, go to Yahoo.com and choose stock quotes. Enter the ticker symbol for the company you are interested in, and Yahoo will provide its most recent press releases, which will include past quarterly and annual reports with the financial statements.

You can also check the previous reports to compare which direction the company is moving in and look for trends (i.e. increasing debt load, unpredictable earnings, decreasing revenues, erratic spending, etc...).

There are also many other Internet resources which provide similar information, which we detail in Chapter Seven, Information Sources.

Comparison Shopping:

To familiarize yourself with some of the numbers, try looking up the financials of three companies you own or are interested in.

• **Balance Sheet:** Which of the companies has the greatest long term debt load? Do any of the companies have greater current liabilities than current assets? Compare the current share price to the shareholder's equity (book value) per share: is the share price much greater or less than the book value?

• **Earnings Statement:** What were the revenues of the most recent year (or quarter) and does the number represent an increase or decrease from the previous period? How much money per share did the company earn (or lose) in the most recent period?

• **Statement of Changes in Financial Position:** Has company debt been increasing or decreasing? What was the greatest expense the company incurred according to the statement?

Decision Making:

Financial statements can provide investors with a partial fundamental snapshot of a company. They only represent one piece of the puzzle. Remember that, while financial statements can help investors compare several companies, that comparison is limited only to the numbers provided.

In other words, you can see that one company made money while the other lost money, but you don't know which has the better technical outlook (based on analysis of the trading chart), which is a potential takeover target, which will have the best future earnings, etc...

As well, the impact of financial statements tends to be long-term as it relates to share prices. Four quarterly reports showing increasing earnings may push the stock into an upward trend as the market begins to recognize the improvements of the underlying company, but one single quarter of increasing earnings may or may not have a significant impact on shares.

Therefore, most investors use financial statements as part of a greater overall decision making process. Certainly, though, an understanding of, and familiarization with, the data can benefit any investor who takes the time to make educated trading decisions.

We suggest using the information you can find in financial statements in combination with **Leeds Analysis** as detailed in Chapter Three.

Important Points:

Many growth companies don't need nor are expected to have positive earnings. Instead, they generally accumulate debt as they focus on research and development of new technologies, aggressively move into new markets, fight for market share with competitors, etc...

Other companies with minimal growth prospects should have more importance placed on actual earnings, lowering operational costs, etc...

Be sure to understand what numbers are important and unimportant to a specific company based on their situation and the sector they are in. This can be done easily by doing an industry comparison on the company in question. Do companies in the same industry or sector seem to have positive earnings, or is the focus on growth, research, etc... Are they a larger or smaller company than the industry average, and are they growing faster than the others?

Read the fine print to make sure the numbers you are reading have been audited, rather than being just company estimates, or unverified results. This generally is not something you need to worry about with most exchange-listed companies, but it is important practice.

Many annual statements will begin with positive news about sales or revenue increases, or other positive comments, but further reading reveals that the company actually lost money, increased debt, or had a poor quarter or year. For most companies their financial statements are part of their promotional material and they need to make the information sound as impressive and positive as possible, even if the overall results were disappointing.

Be wary of one-time earnings or losses. For example, a company may win a huge lawsuit settlement and the influx of money gives them positive earnings for the quarter. However, how would they have done when the one-time extraordinary gain is ignored?

Bonus Chapter:
Halts and Delistings

Listing Status:

To maintain exchange-listed status, a company must meet certain minimum standards. Failure to do so can result in delisting; meaning shares are no longer traded on that exchange. Delisted stocks can still trade on alternative markets (OTC, pink sheets), but these markets enforce less-stringent standards, creating a riskier environment for investors.

(Learn more about the various penny stock markets in Chapter Two, in the section entitled **Where Do Penny Stocks Trade**?)

A stock trades on one of these exchanges only after a company has met an exchange's listing requirements, which are set by its board of governors. Requirements vary, but generally include net-worth minimums, number of shareholders, pre-tax income or revenues, and rules regarding corporate governance and public disclosure of financial statements. In addition, companies pay tens of thousands of dollars a year in tiered annual fees in order to be listed.

The listing process was established to help create fair markets and protect investors from fraud and stock manipulation. The National Association of Securities Dealers (NASD) was created by the Securities and Exchange Commission to ensure fair trading practices.

Exchange listing assures investors that a company has met certain financial criteria. It is also a frequent prerequisite for a company to sell its shares to such institutional investors as pension funds and endowments. Association with an exchange can attract the attention of research analysts and lend prestige to a company.

Delisting:

For a variety of reasons, companies may fall off/get booted from an exchange. Generally this occurs due to lack of compliance with the rules, mergers, acquisitions, bankruptcies or even something criminal such as fraud.

On the NYSE and AMEX, delistings occur relatively rarely.

Estimates from the AMEX show that the exchange loses 40 stocks a year.

Recent regulatory reforms have pushed delistings on the NASDAQ to record levels. According to the NASD, about 2,000 stocks have fallen off the NASDAQ since 1997, when the NASD adopted tighter financial requirements and a $1 minimum bid (no other exchange requires a minimum stock price). The new standards were adopted in response to growing concerns from the SEC about full and adequate disclosure of company information, fraud and stock-price manipulation.

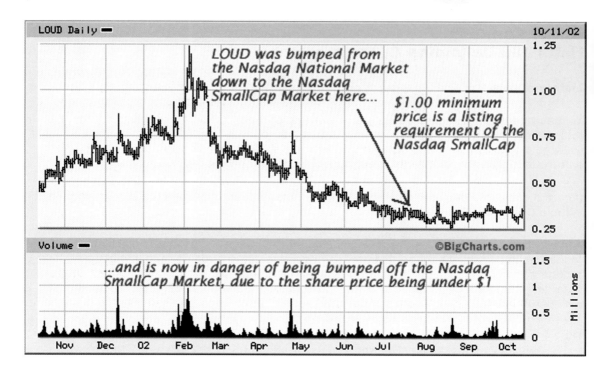

LOUD Daily ▬   10/11/02

LOUD was bumped from the Nasdaq National Market down to the Nasdaq SmallCap Market here...

$1.00 minimum price is a listing requirement of the Nasdaq SmallCap

...and is now in danger of being bumped off the Nasdaq SmallCap Market, due to the share price being under $1

Volume ▬   ©BigCharts.com

Nov   Dec   02   Feb   Mar   Apr   May   Jun   Jul   Aug   Sep   Oct

NASDAQ officials say the $1 minimum bid is one of the most common reasons for delisting. If a company's share price falls below $1 for 30 consecutive trading days, it may be delisted. Most stocks delisted from the NASDAQ National Market resume trading on the NASDAQ SmallCap Market.

Once a company is notified by an exchange that it is at risk of delisting, it may request a hearing to allow it time to return to good standing.

Alternative Markets:

Companies delisted from the major exchanges may end up trading on one of two over-the-counter markets:

The OTC Bulletin Board: The OTC-BB, which is also run by the NASD, is relatively non-liquid compared to the three major exchanges. For example, in May 1998, about half of the market's roughly 6,500 issues traded at less than 50 cents a share, and fewer than half traded in that month, according to the OTCBB.

Historically, companies trading on the OTCBB were not required to file regular financial statements with regulators. This removed a cumbersome ritual for small, closely held public companies that didn't care if their shares were actively traded. However, the NASD adopted rules in 1999 requiring filing for all companies trading in this market.

Pink Sheets: Many companies that fall off the OTCBB are likely to land on the Pink Sheets. The National Quotation Bureau, a private company in New York, runs this market. Each day, information on some 3,000 stocks is printed on sheets of pink paper and sent to paid subscribers (mostly brokerage houses).

Since the Pink Sheets don't require any financial reporting, it is generally considered the last stop for companies that have nowhere else to trade their securities.

Bonus Chapter:
Penny Stock Trading Considerations

There are many differences between penny stocks and other types of investments, which means that your investment approach towards penny stocks must be adapted accordingly.

Large Price Spread:

The difference between the bid and the ask price is generally greater for small cap stocks.

This is due to two factors:

1. Fewer parties are involved in the trading of penny stock shares.

2. Appropriate valuations are much more difficult to estimate for penny stock companies.

The spread between bid and ask prices for small cap stocks can often be greater than 10%, so it is very important to use a LIMIT order rather than a MARKET order, so as to ensure the trading price of the shares you buy or sell.

Volatility:

Penny stocks are often very volatile and can make large percentage moves in short time frames. This means that investors should keep a watchful eye on their investments, rather than buying and holding for the long term. While there are many penny stocks available which may be long term investments, they still need to be monitored very closely due to their volatility.

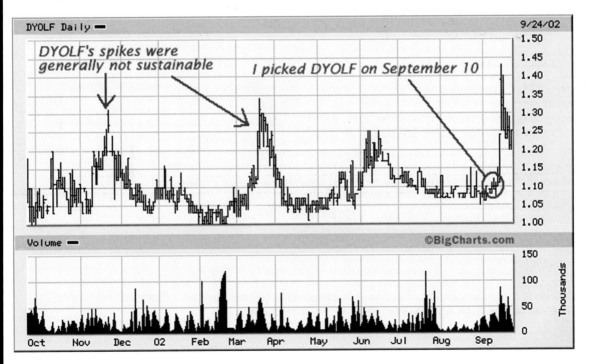

Conventional Rules Don't Always Apply:

Forces driving penny stocks are very different than those affecting the share prices of other types of investments. For example, speculation, promotional efforts, seasonality, and 'potential' are a few criteria which should be examined in greater depth with penny stocks than other investments.

As well, depending on the type of company, patents and technological innovations, success of surrounding exploration claims, past management effectiveness, and corporate alliances can also play a major role in the direction of the share price.

While other criteria do apply, such as technical indicators, standard fundamental analysis, insider trading, and institutional sponsorship, they impact the underlying stock differently depending if it is a small company or a large company.

Takeover and Acquisition Targets:

The smaller relative size of many penny stock companies makes them more likely to be taken over by larger companies in the same industry.

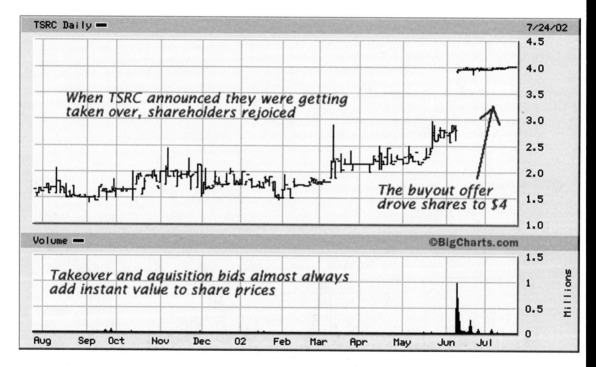

As well, many smaller companies have the rights to important exploration lands, technology patents, or strategic market share which they don't have the resources to effectively exploit, meaning that larger corporations can move in and benefit where the smaller company was unable to.

When a company gets taken over it is usually to the benefit of the shareholders, as they often realize a price increase in their holdings.

Investor Expectations:

The reasons for investing in penny stocks generally involve the hope of large, significant profit. The average investor will hold their shares in a penny stock company for shorter time periods than they would for a blue chip corporation, and will hold out for significant profits before selling their shares. This is important to consider when gaining an understanding of investor sentiment towards a particular company, and extrapolating share price movements from that understanding.

Investor expectations are also different as they relate to company operations. It is generally more acceptable for a small cap company to be losing money, over-spending on research and development, or growing very rapidly.

It is less than acceptable from an investor's point of view for a penny stock company to be undergoing negative or nil growth, to be paying dividends, or to be diversifying among non-related industries.

Bonus Chapter:
Past Penny Stock Trends

In the quest for easy money, society has continually put themselves on the line.

Despite the fact that they get burned almost all of the time, people seem to purposefully forget past lessons. Perhaps they are just that forgetful, but I doubt it. More likely they are willing to take the gamble for the fun of it, or are afraid of missing the boat that others are piling onto.

The dot-com bubble which burst in the first quarter of the year 2000 was a prime example. Many penny stocks were exploding in price simply because they were penny stocks.

Here is a prime example of how stocks were spiking in the first three months of 2000.

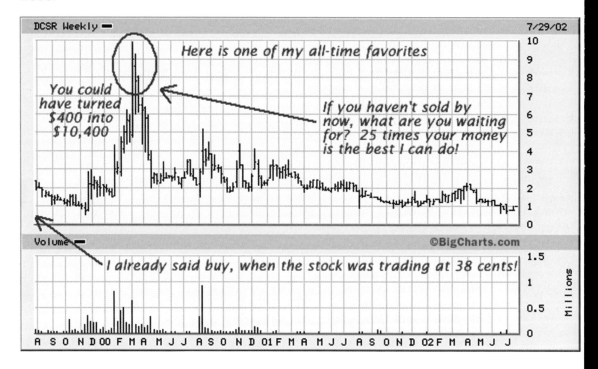

In a four month period at the end of 1999 and the beginning of 2000, I personally realized over a 100% gain in my total trading portfolio. On January 4, 2000, I published a report to subscribers of PeterLeeds.com entitled "NASDAQ Warning Signs" to warn them of the coming collapse. I must admit that very few people listened to my comments.

However, I certainly do not blame them. With every top-notch analyst and brokerage house screaming about the next amazing IPO, and even your grandmother calling you up to tell you her latest hot stock tip, how could you, or anyone else, sit out of the frenzy?

Now, the dot-com bubble was not contained to penny stocks, and in general actually applied more to mid and large-cap stocks. Here is a famous example, Nortel, which sank with the rest of the market when the bubble burst, and never recovered.

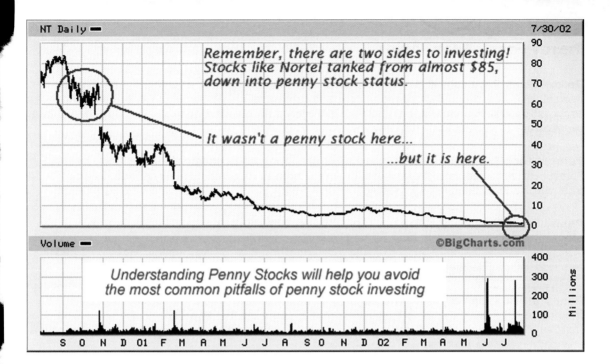

However, the trickle down effect was even more evident in penny stock shares, and the bursting of the bubble just as calamitous.

It was not long until the bubble burst, but it was still two months later than I had expected.

Had a lesson been learned? I say no. Perhaps in the short-term people will avoid getting burned again in the same way, but five or ten years from now I would not be at all surprised to see a repeat of the fiasco.

Will it all happen again?

Absolutely.

Bonus Chapter:
Penny Stock Prophecies

Penny Stock Prophecy # 1: Penny stocks, seen more and more as a legitimate investment vehicle, will gain in popularity among new and less experienced traders. While the negative connotations will remain among Wall Street big-wigs and institutional investors, there will be a silent strata of society that routinely makes quiet profits in penny stocks.

Penny Stock Prophecy # 2: Through tools like *Understanding Penny Stocks* and PeterLeeds.com, regular investors will finally be able to learn about, understand, and profit from the world of penny stock trading.

Penny Stock Prophecy # 3: Investors will be better able to protect themselves from common pitfalls in penny stock investing, due to an increase in the wealth of knowledge on the topic. They will also be able to avoid 'pretenders' selling their unenlightened stock picks, and skirt around dangerous investments more easily.

Penny Stock Prophecy # 4: The majority of penny stock traders will fail to enlighten themselves by taking the time to read information sources like *Understanding Penny Stocks*. Instead they will anxiously dump money onto those shares they hear about at work, or from a friend, or read in a chat room. They will lose money.

Penny Stock Prophecy # 5: Reporting requirements and available information on penny stock companies will become somewhat more readily available. However, the total amount of information will still fall short of what is present for more conventional and commonly held equities, and will also fall short of what would best help individual investors to research their own penny stocks.

Penny Stock Prophecy # 6: Within five to eight years, the stock market will end its upcoming bull run temporarily, and enter another bear market. As the five to eight years progress, penny stock interest and trading activity will both increase, topping out just before the bull run comes to an end. The cycle will repeat.

Penny Stock Prophecy # 7: When another 'dot-com' bubble or Bre-X or Enron surfaces, and it will, the majority of traders will get burned. Meanwhile, a small minority of penny stock traders will make a quiet killing on the underlying stock and you will never hear from them or about them.